Mobile Digital Art:Matter App

by Xiao Chuan Zhou

Mobile Digital Art:Matter App

by Xiao Chuan Zhou

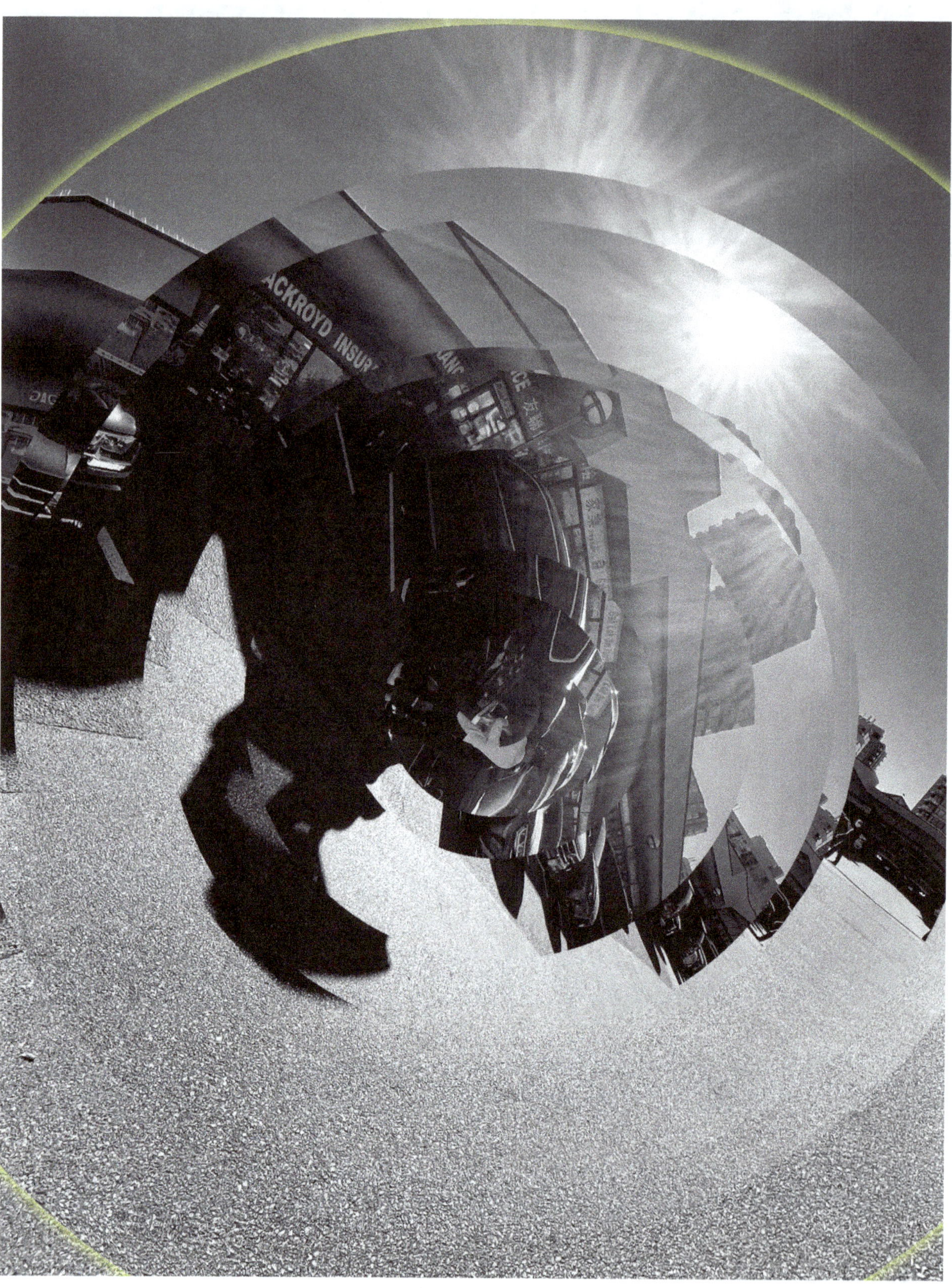
ACKROYD INSUR

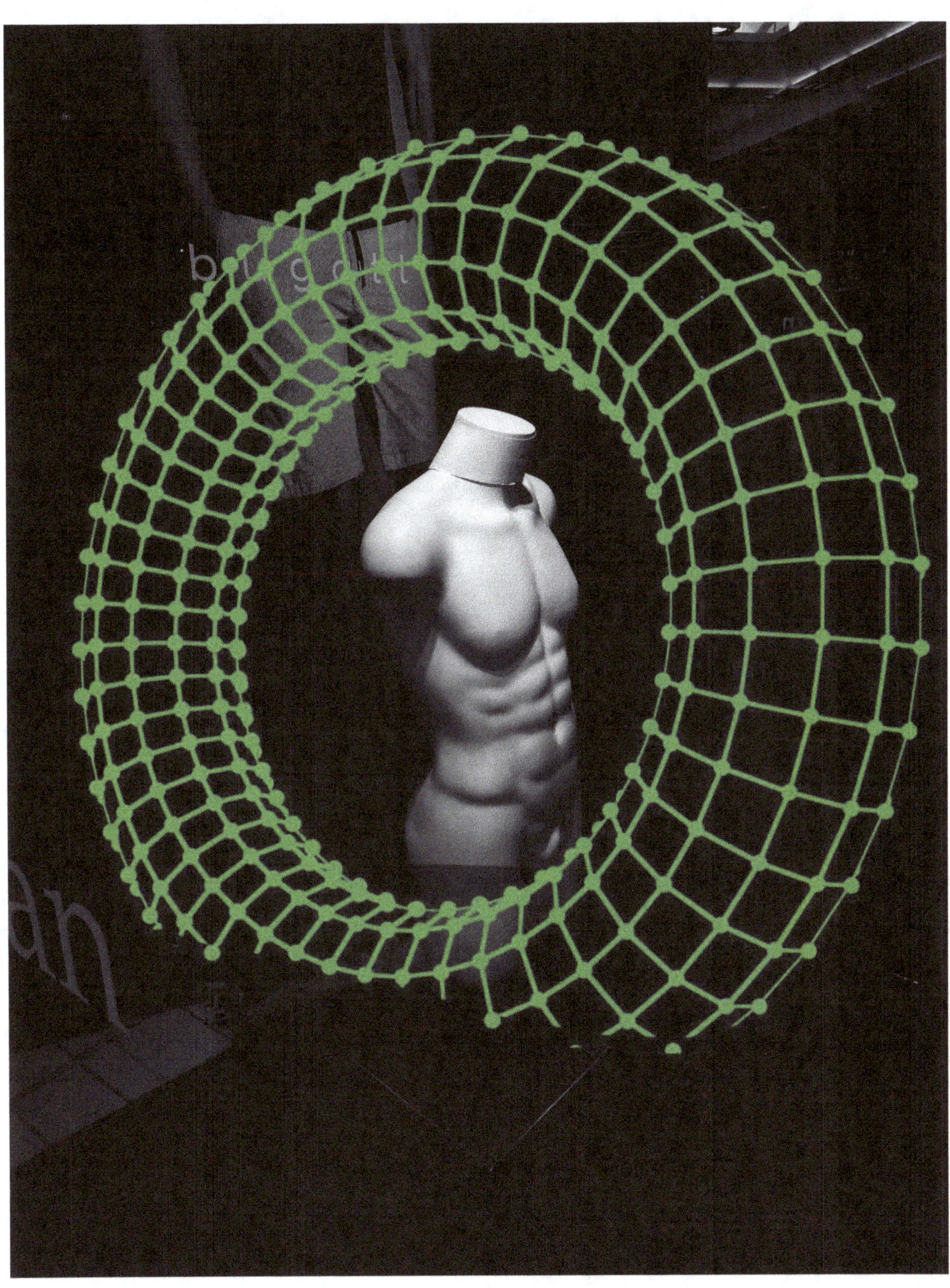

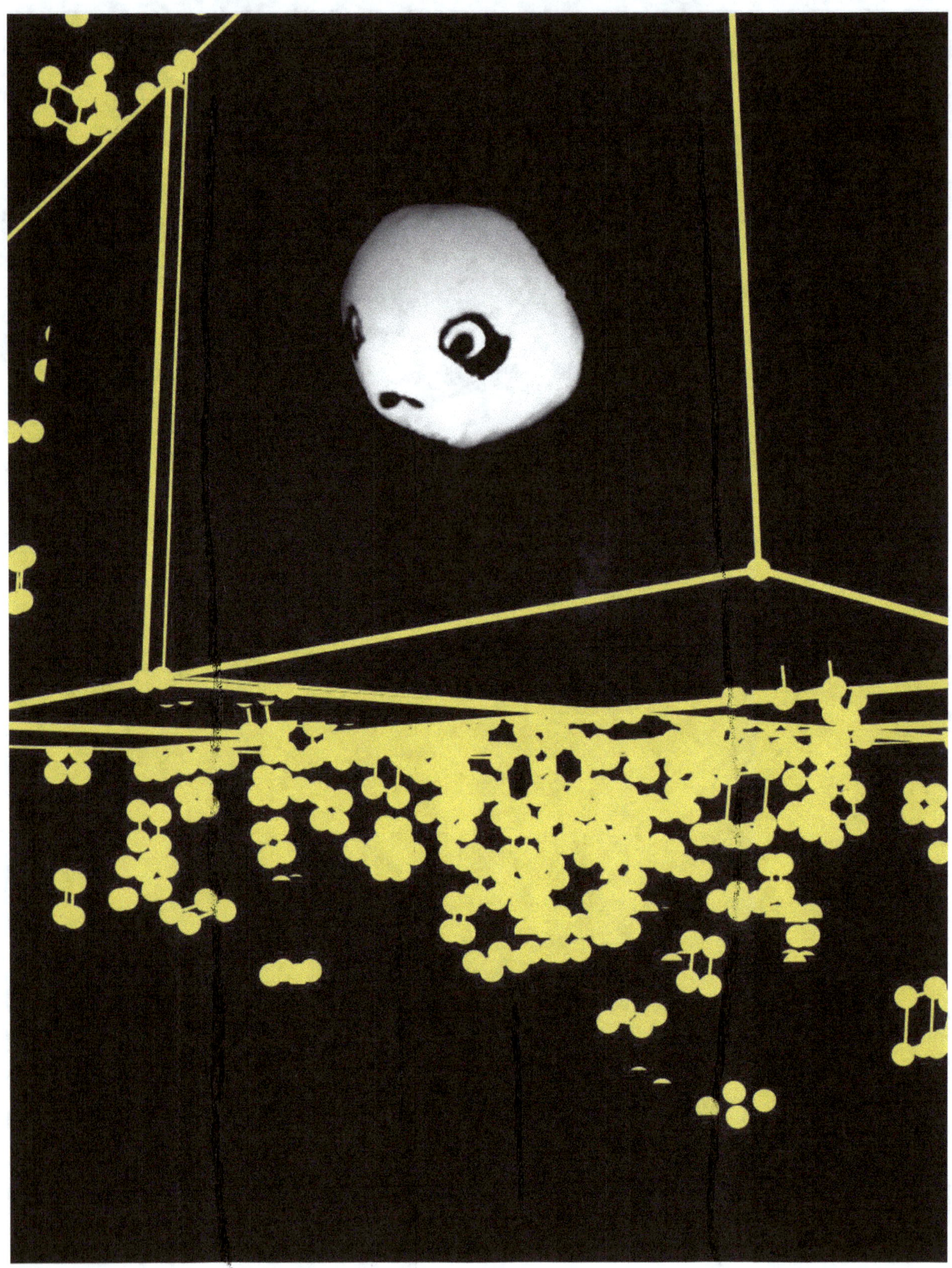

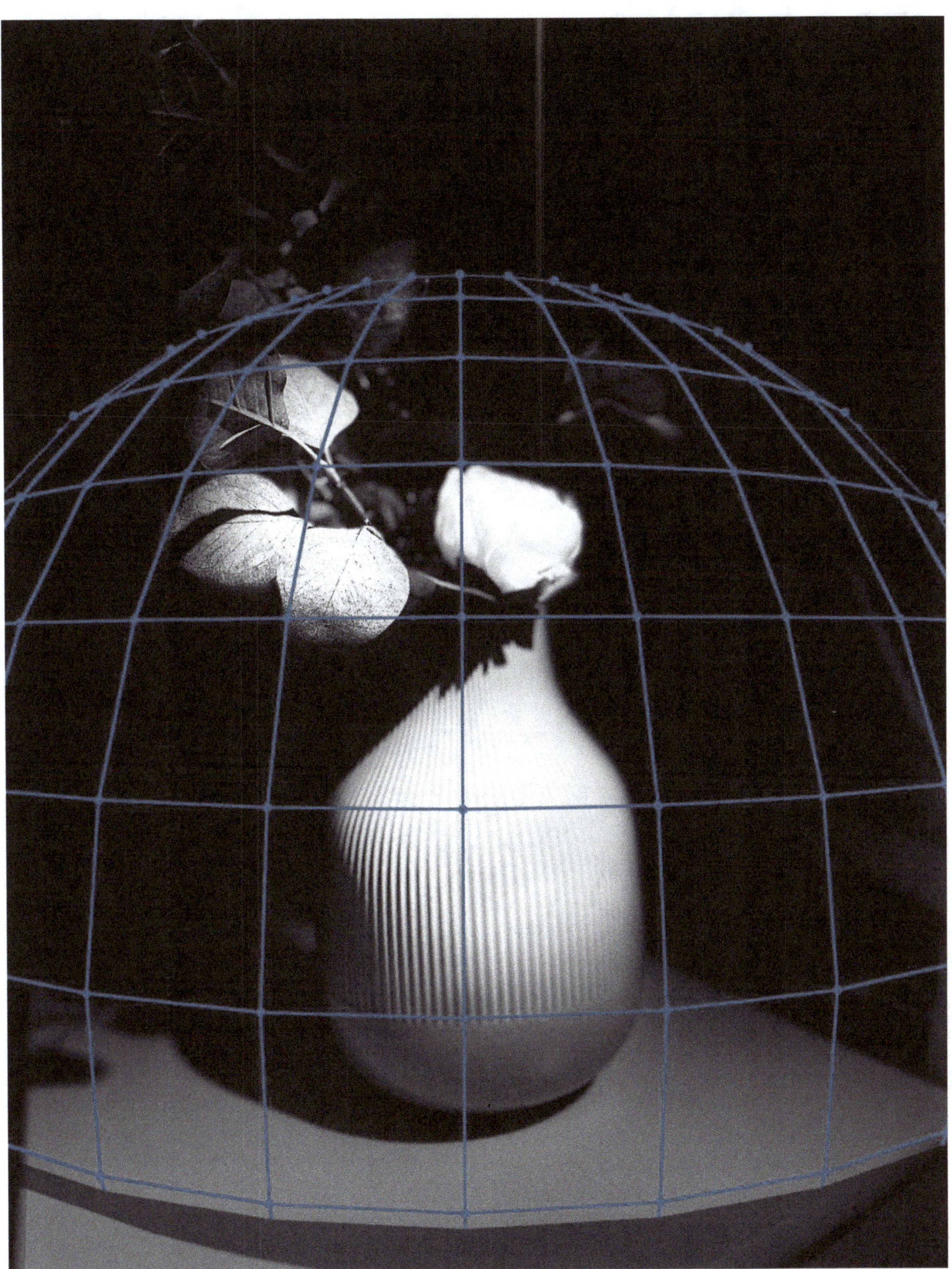

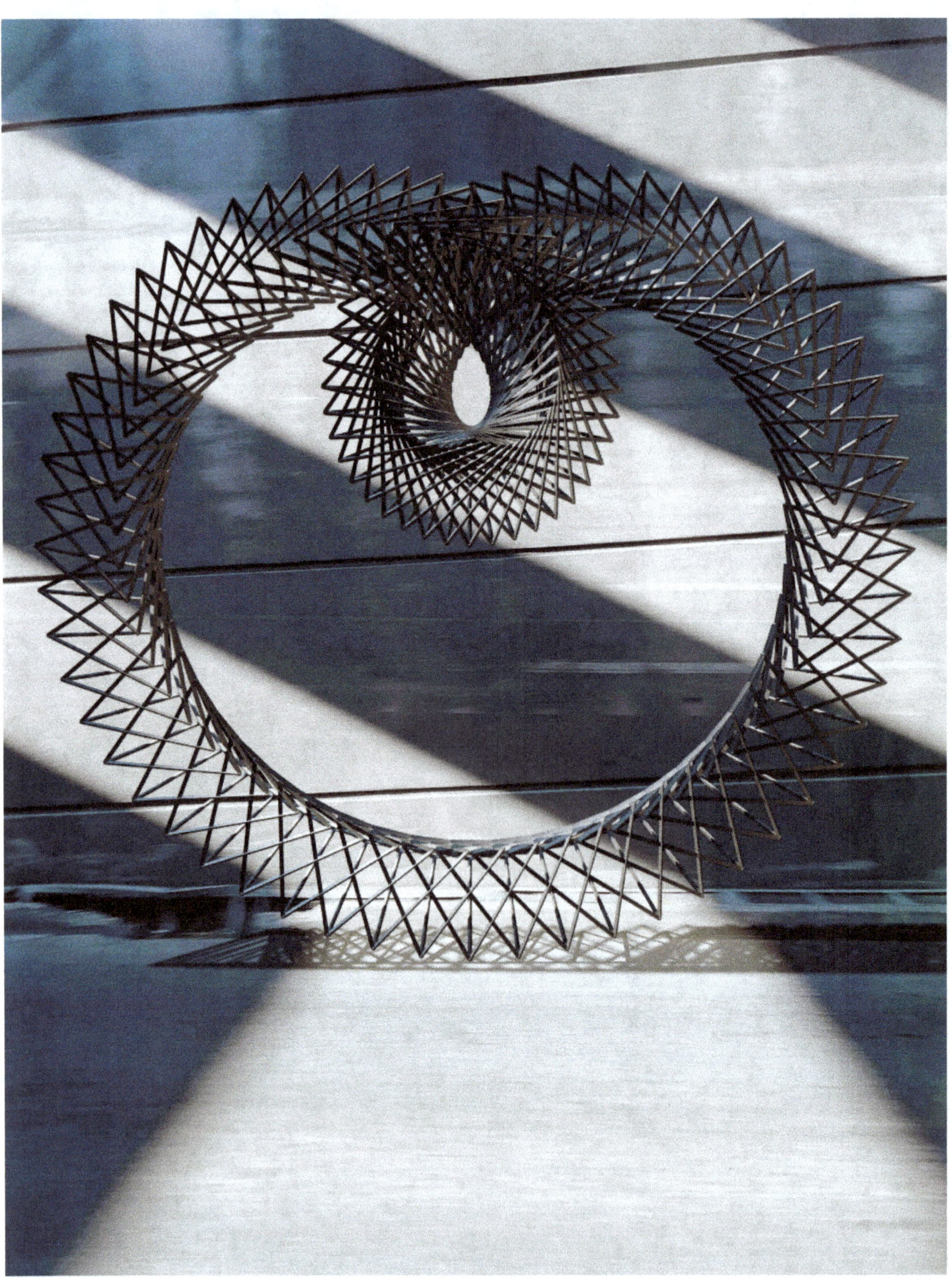

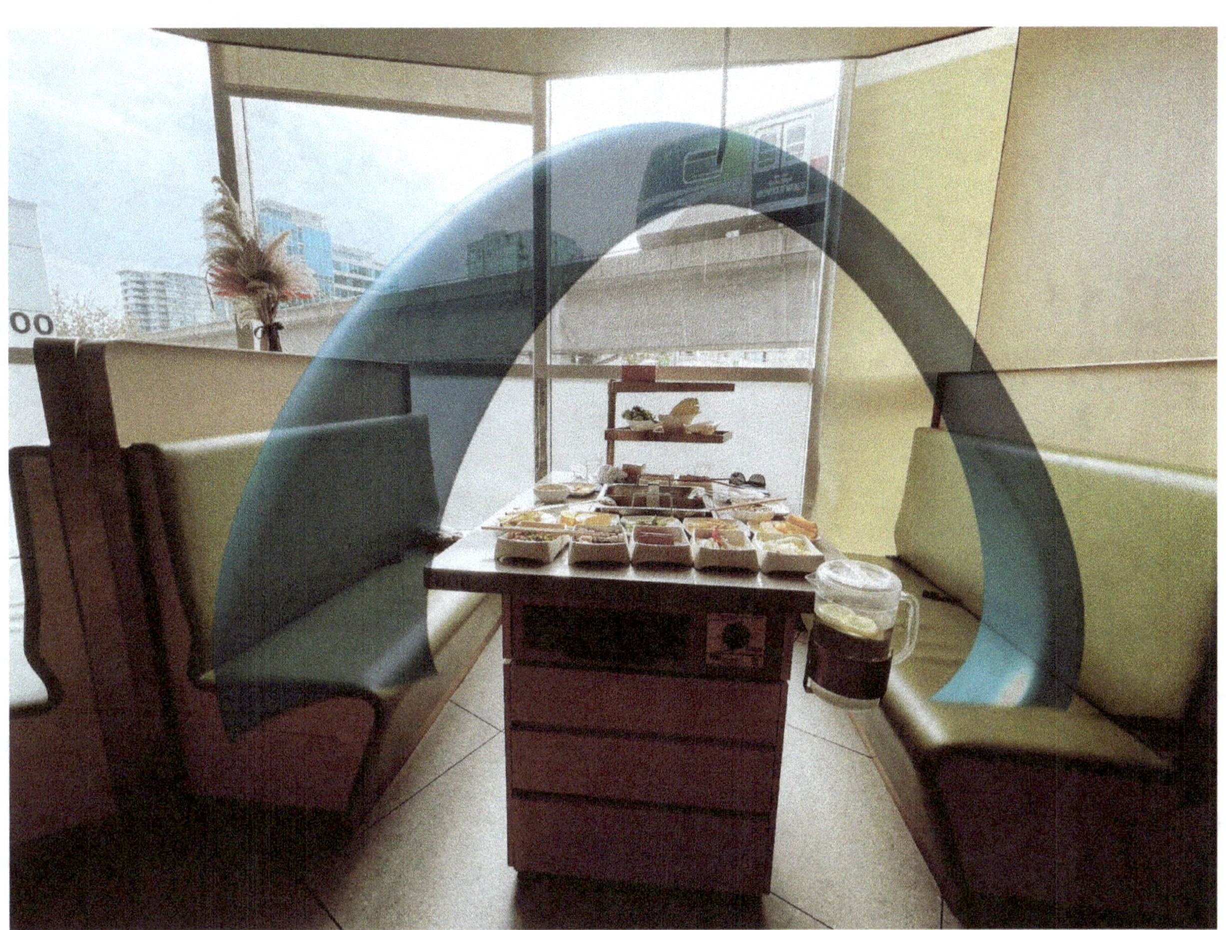

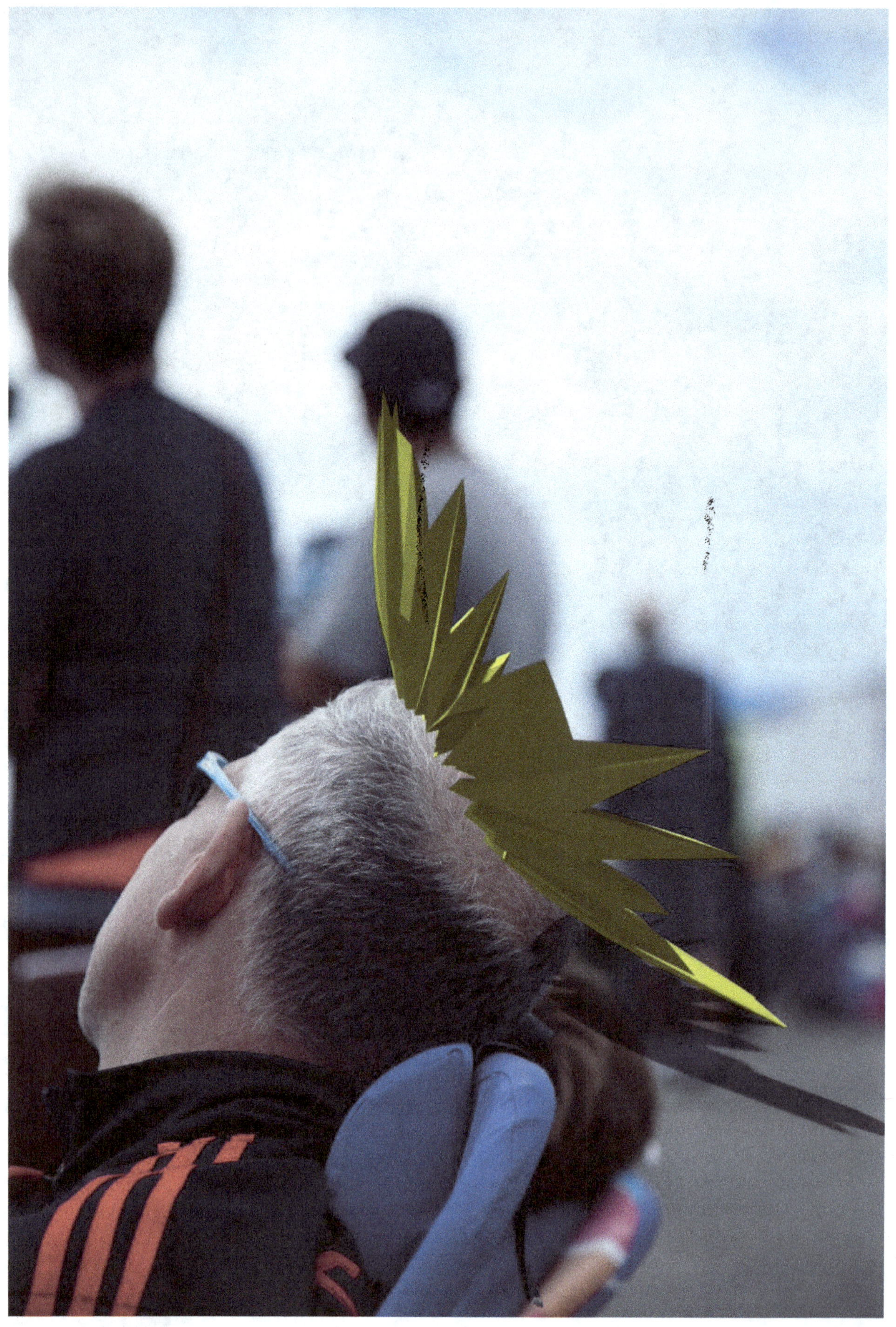

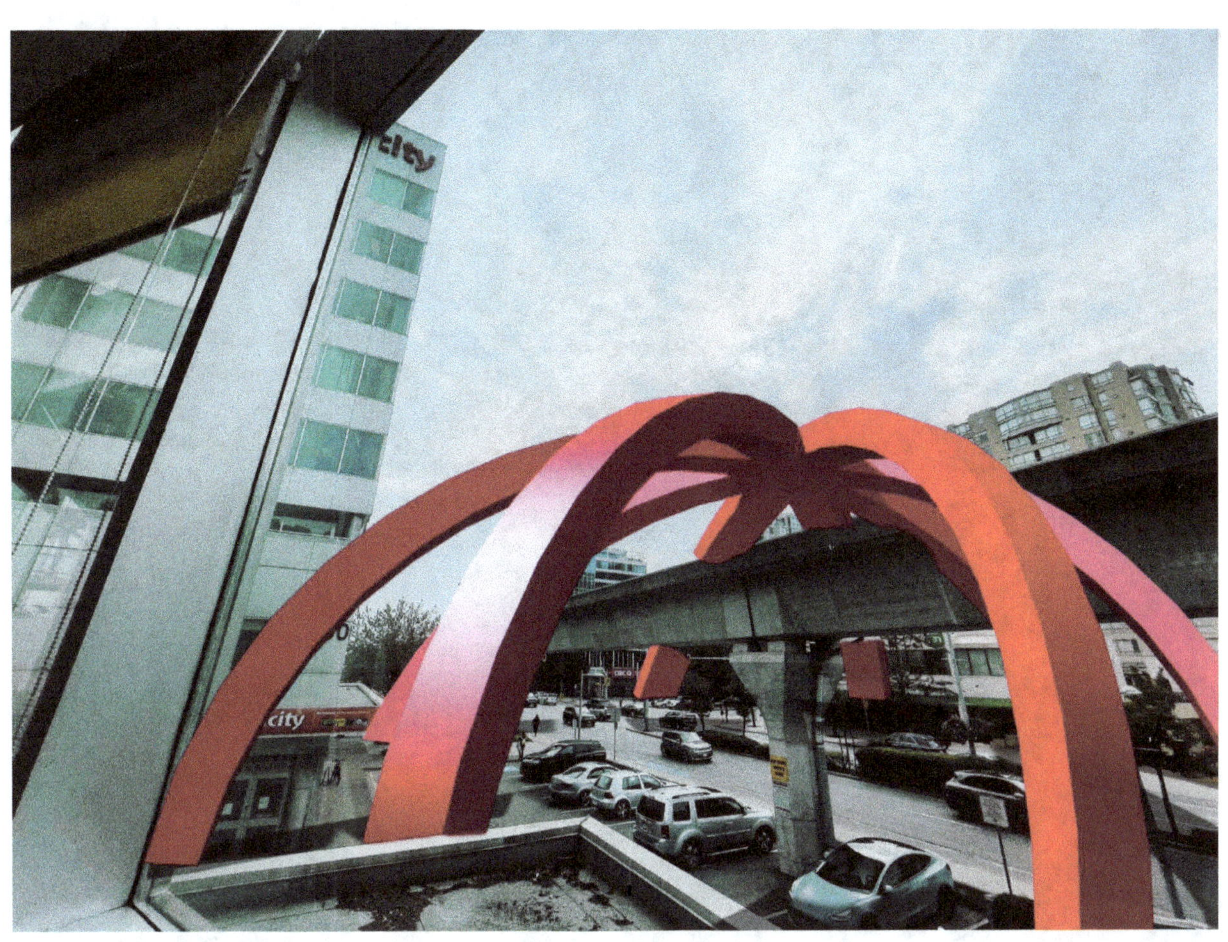

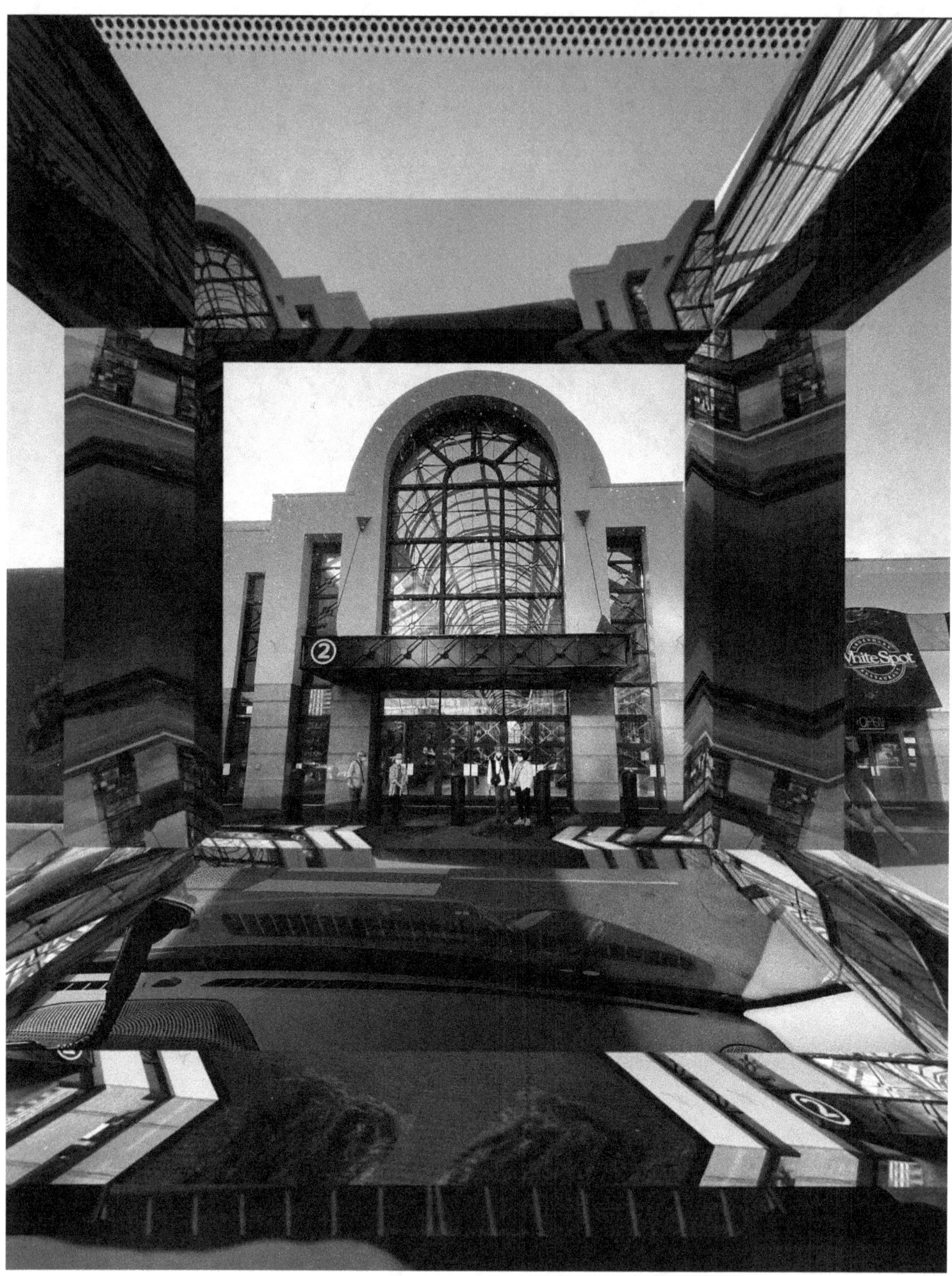
WhiteSpot
OPEN

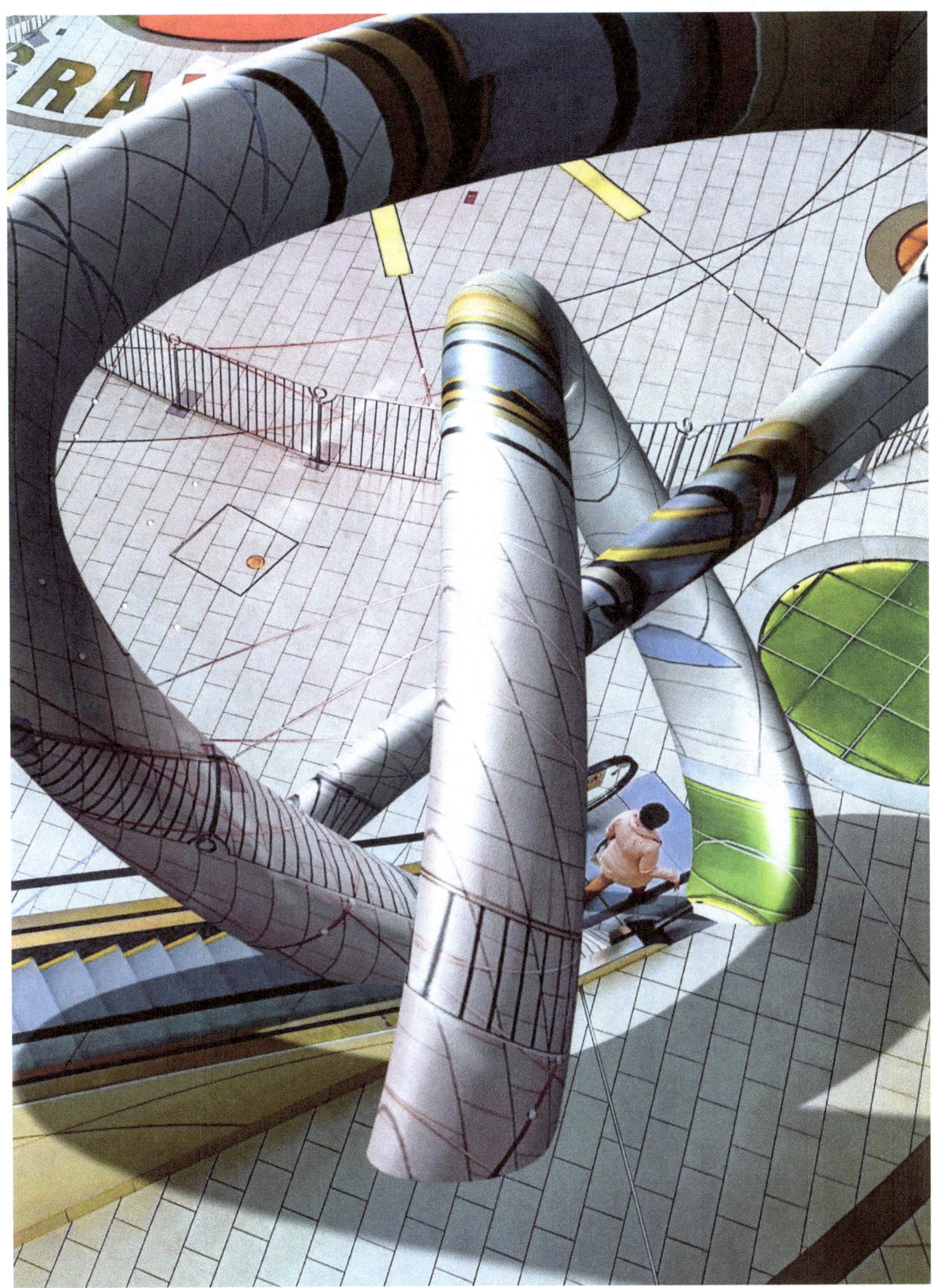
RA

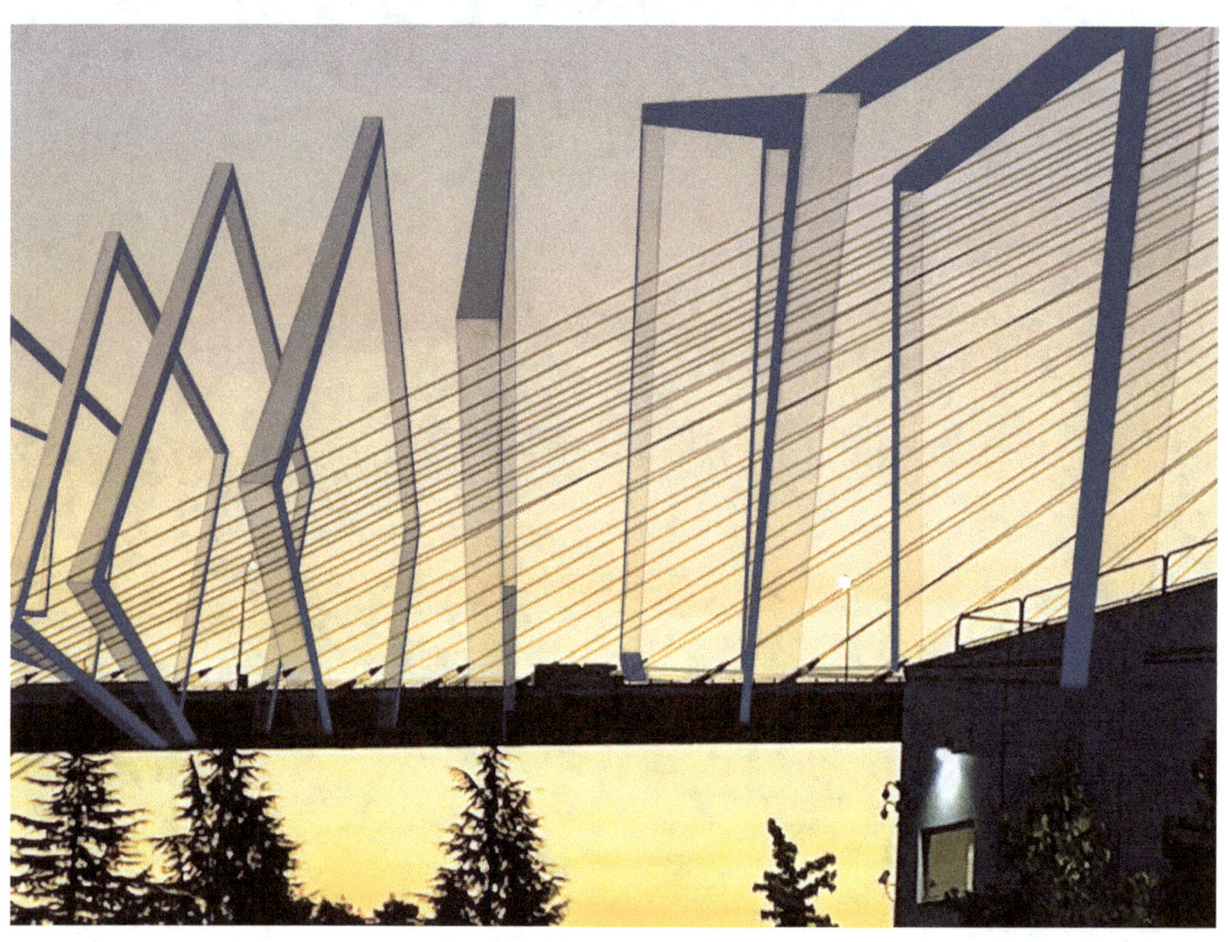

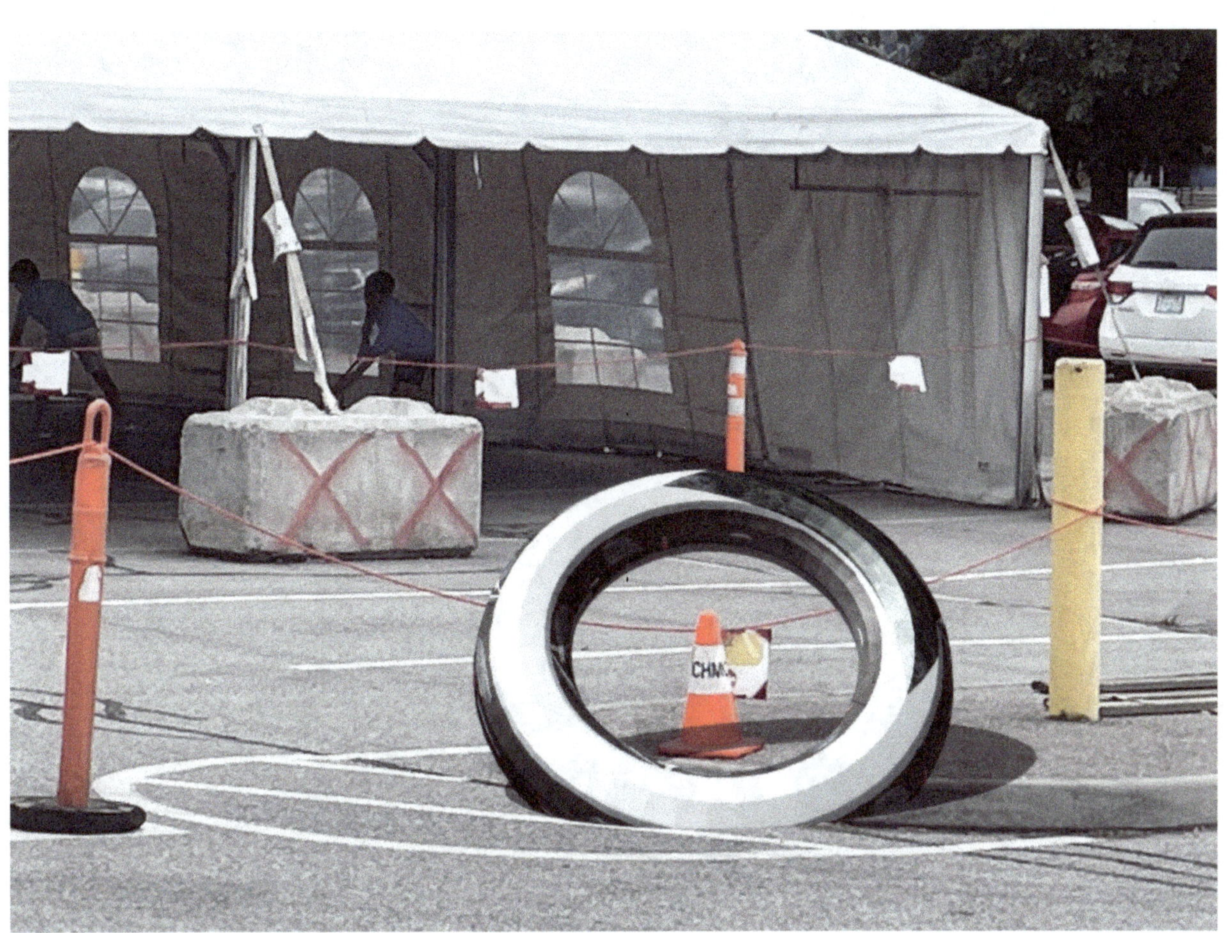
CHM

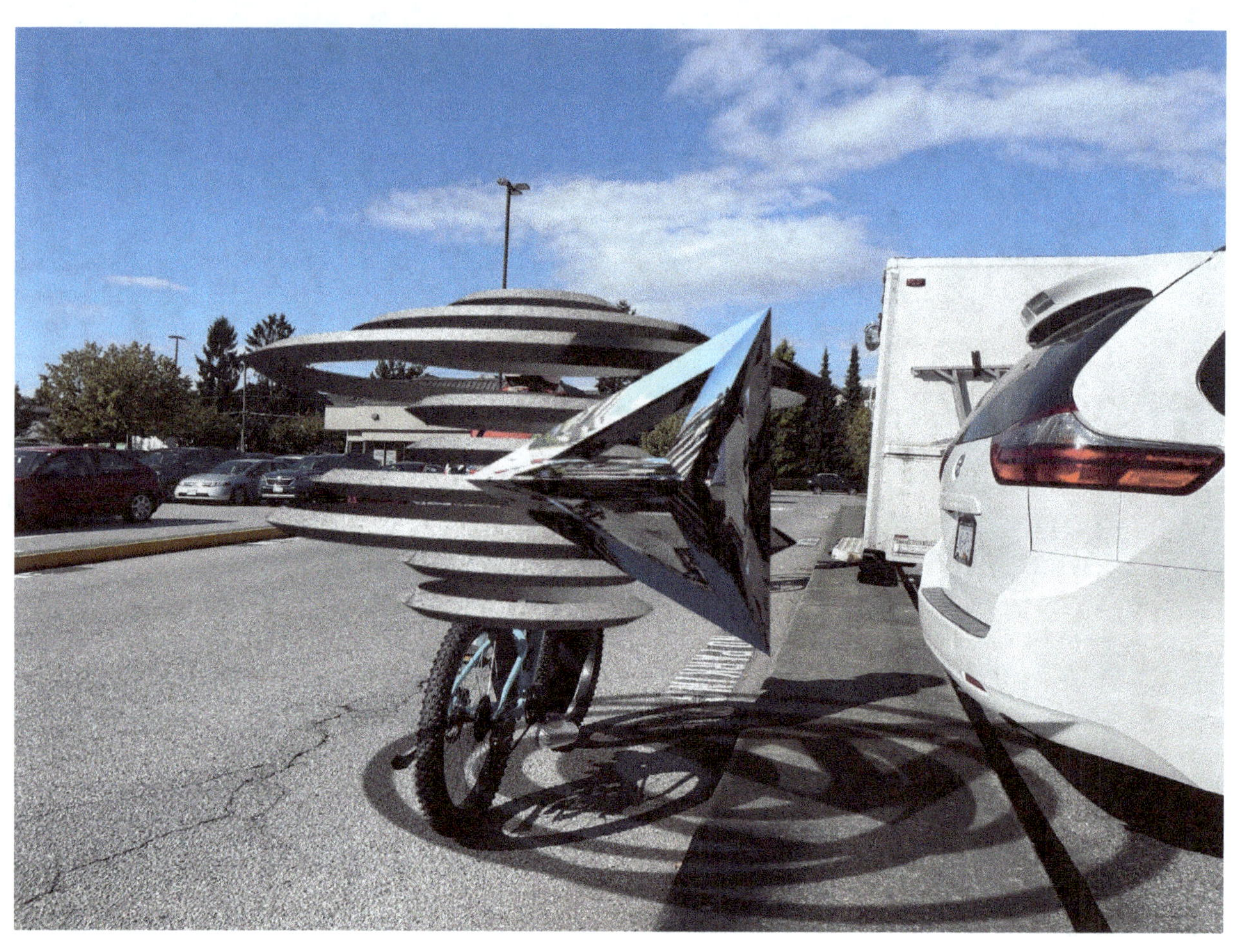

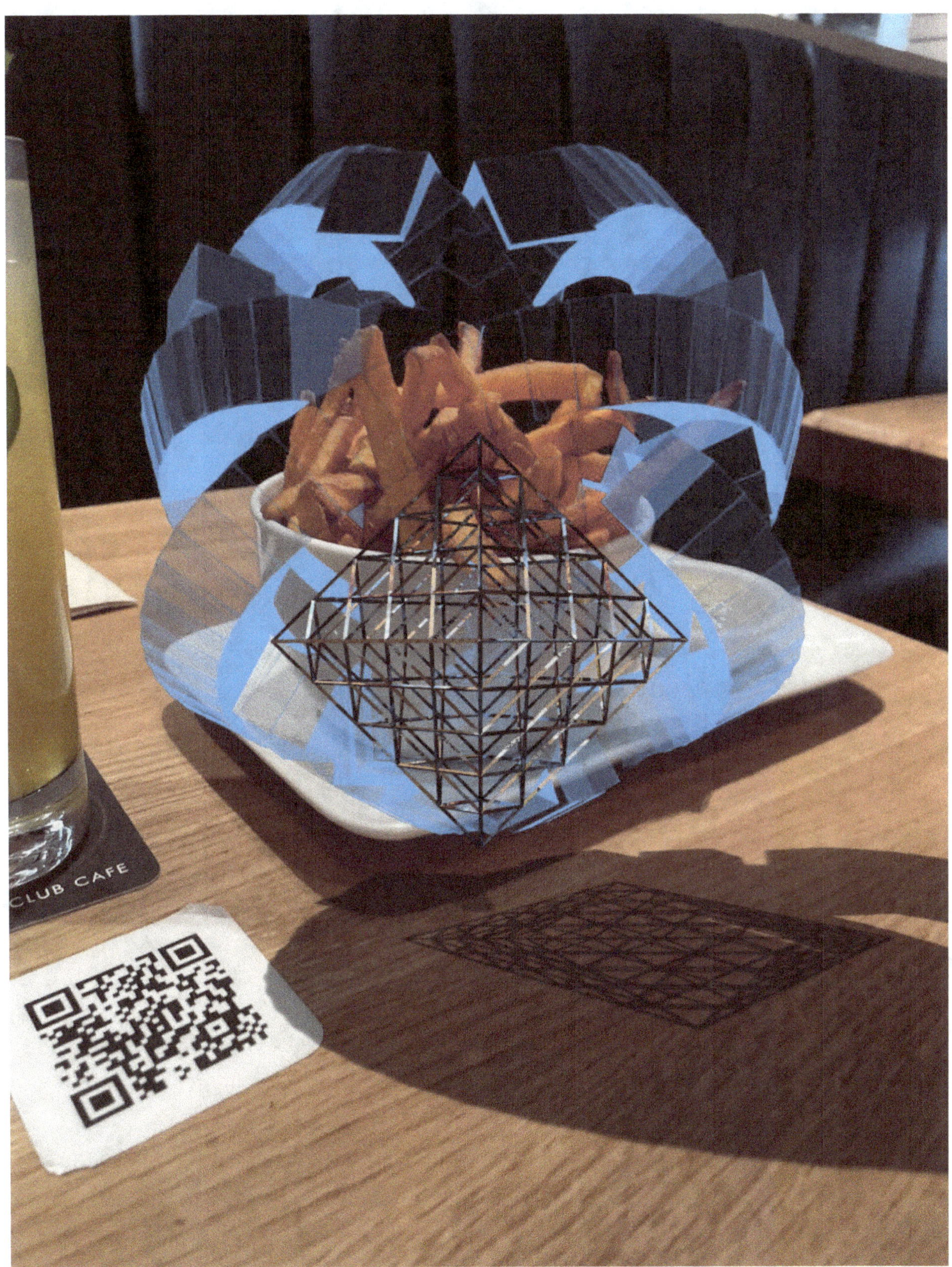
CLUB CAFE

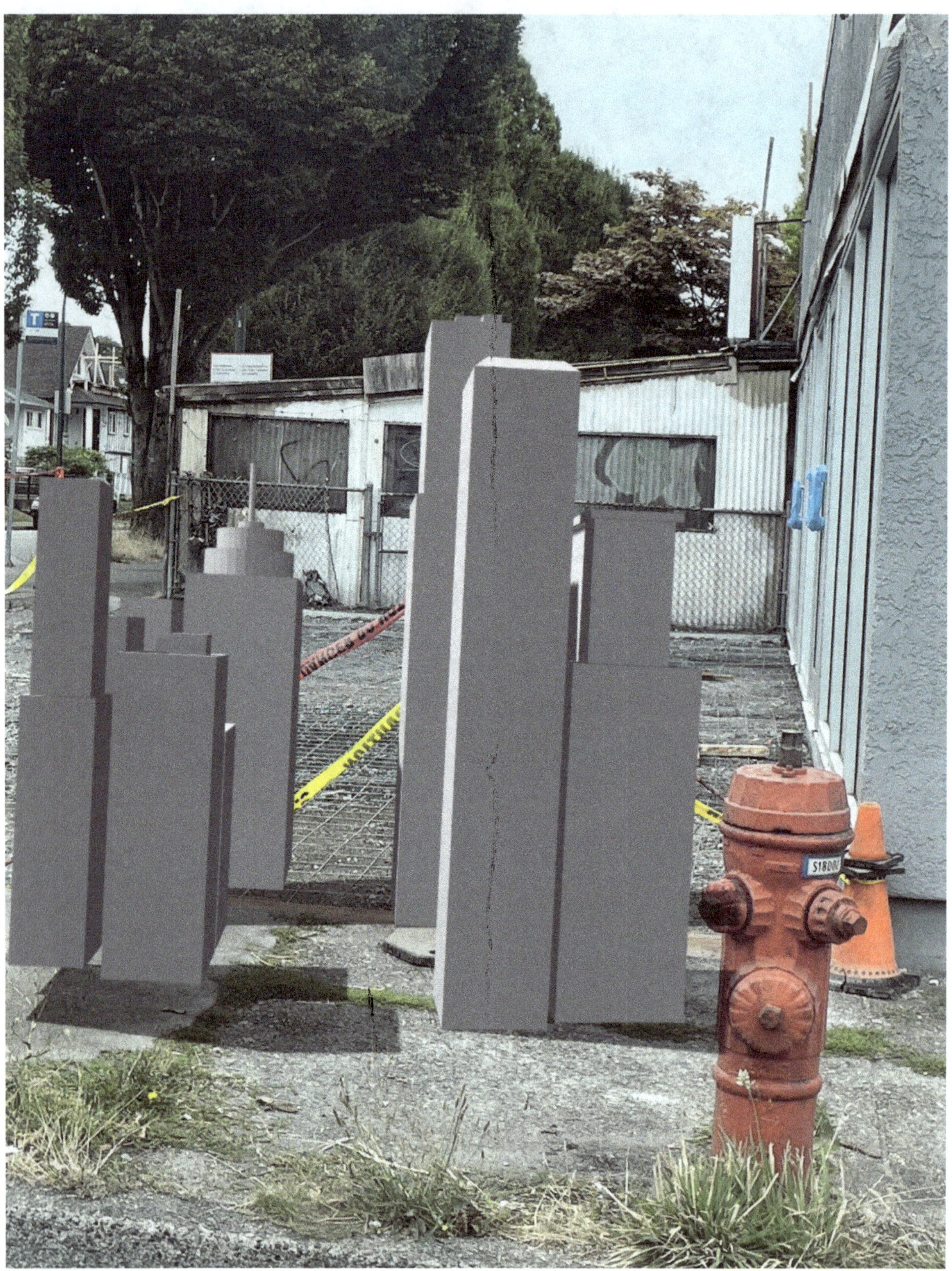

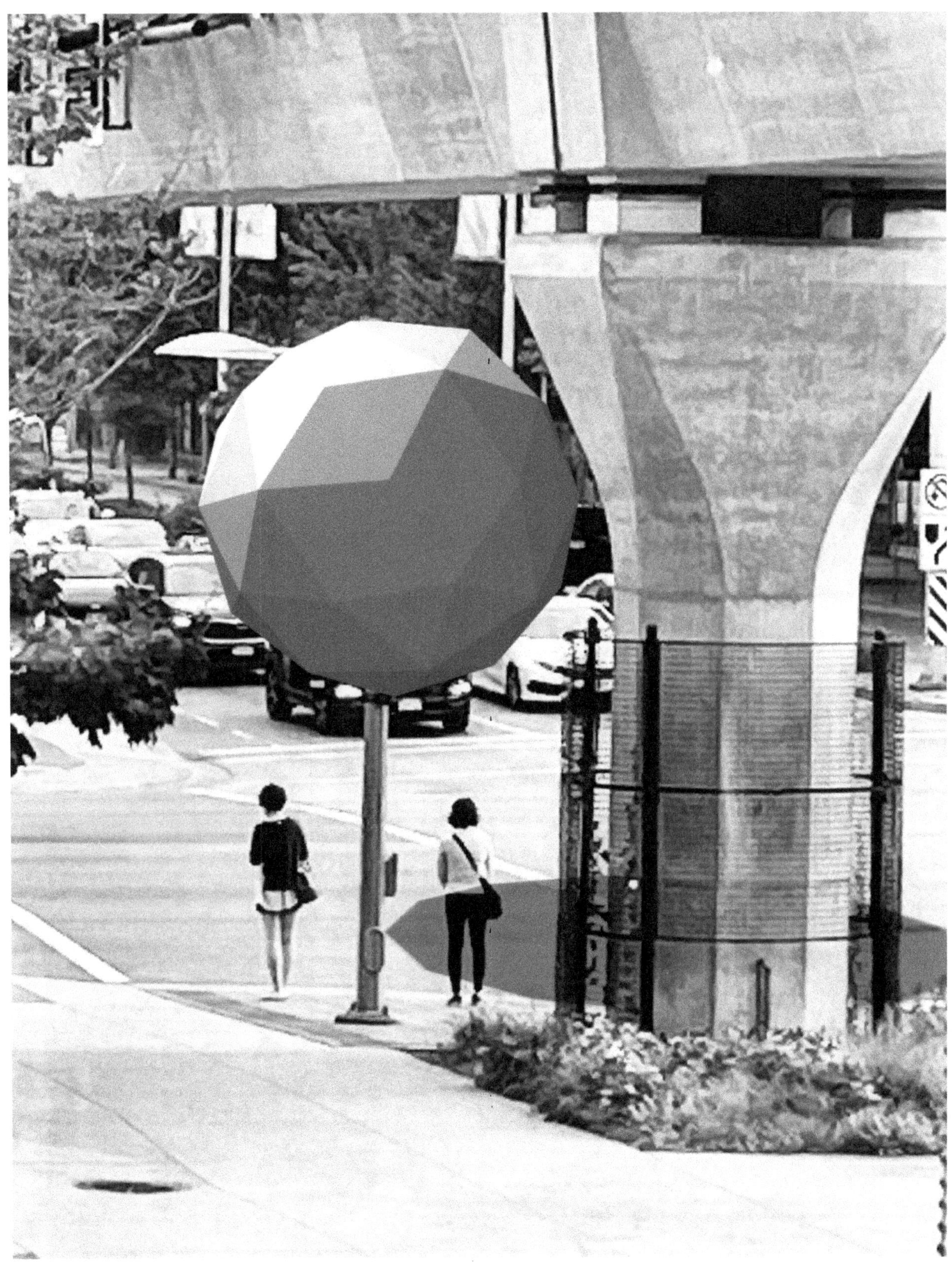

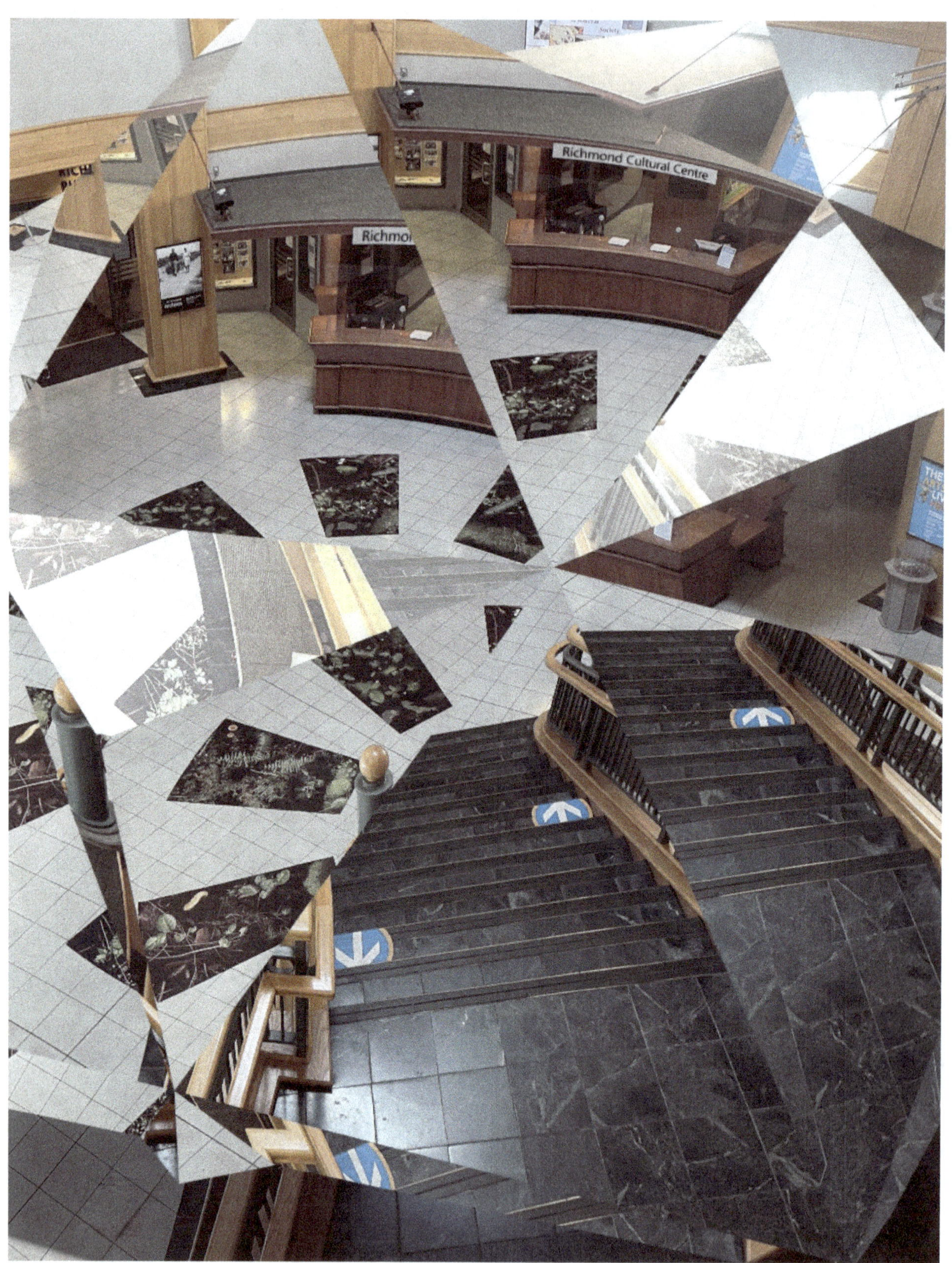
Richmond Cultural Centre
Richmon

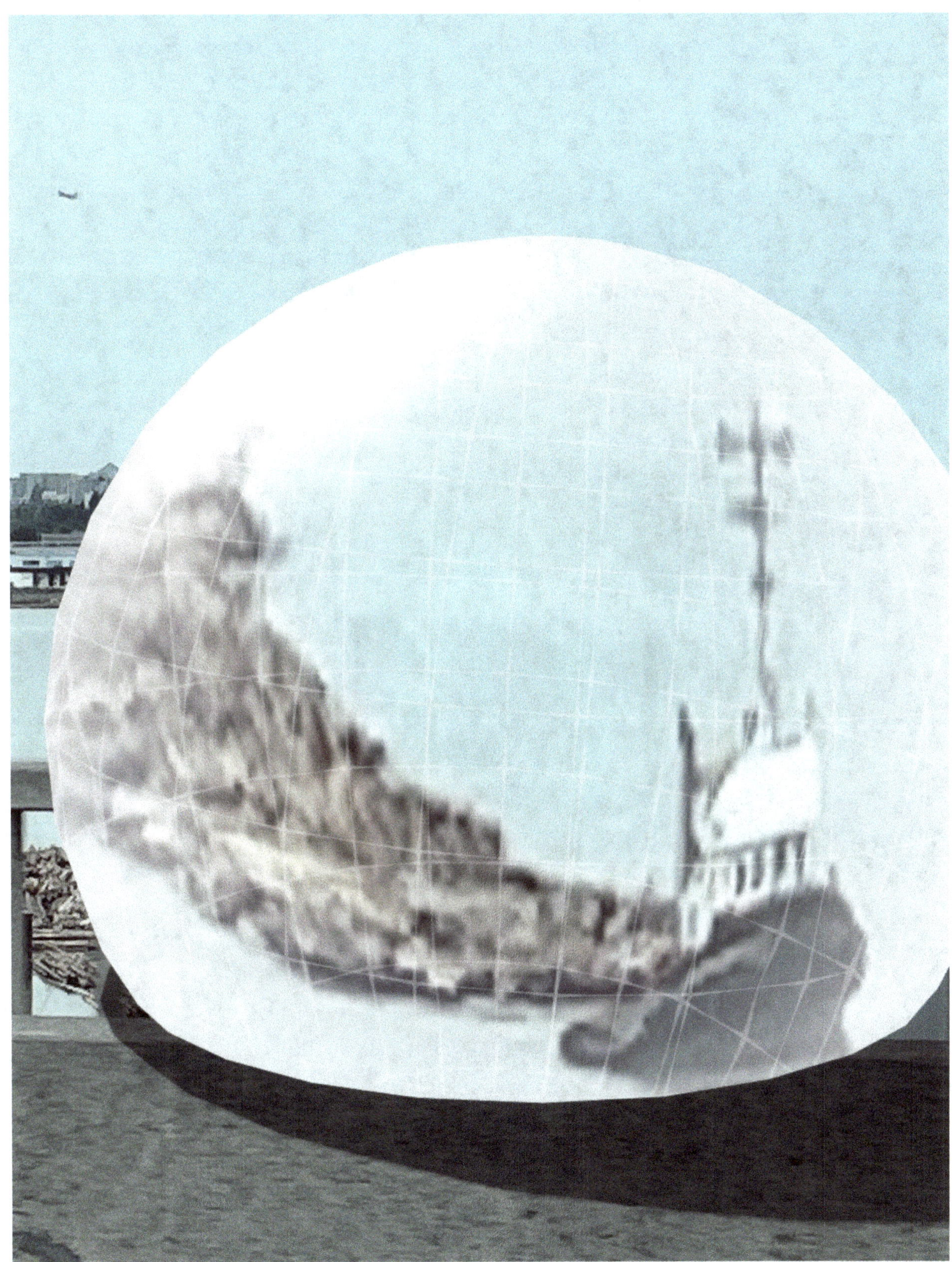

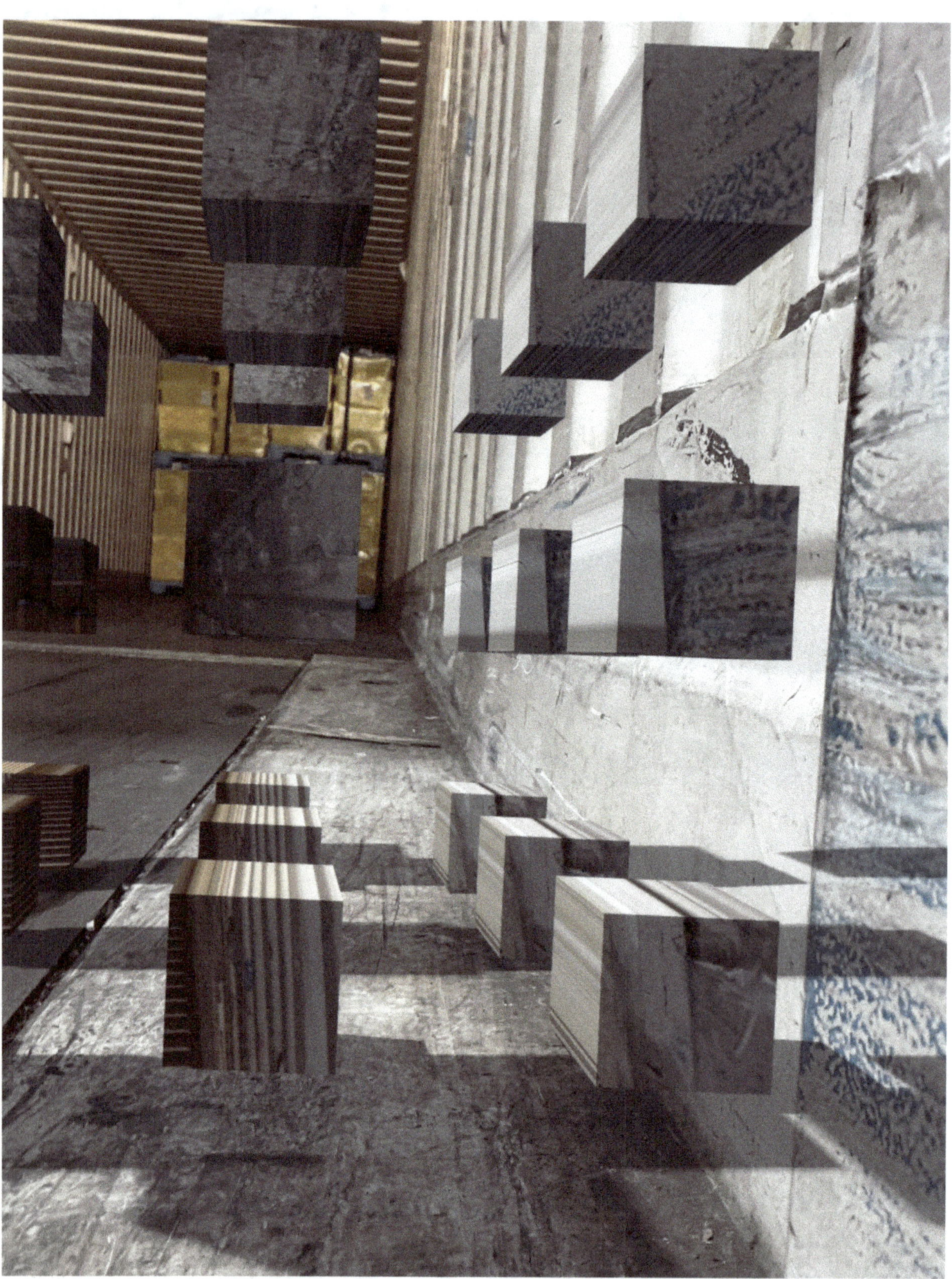

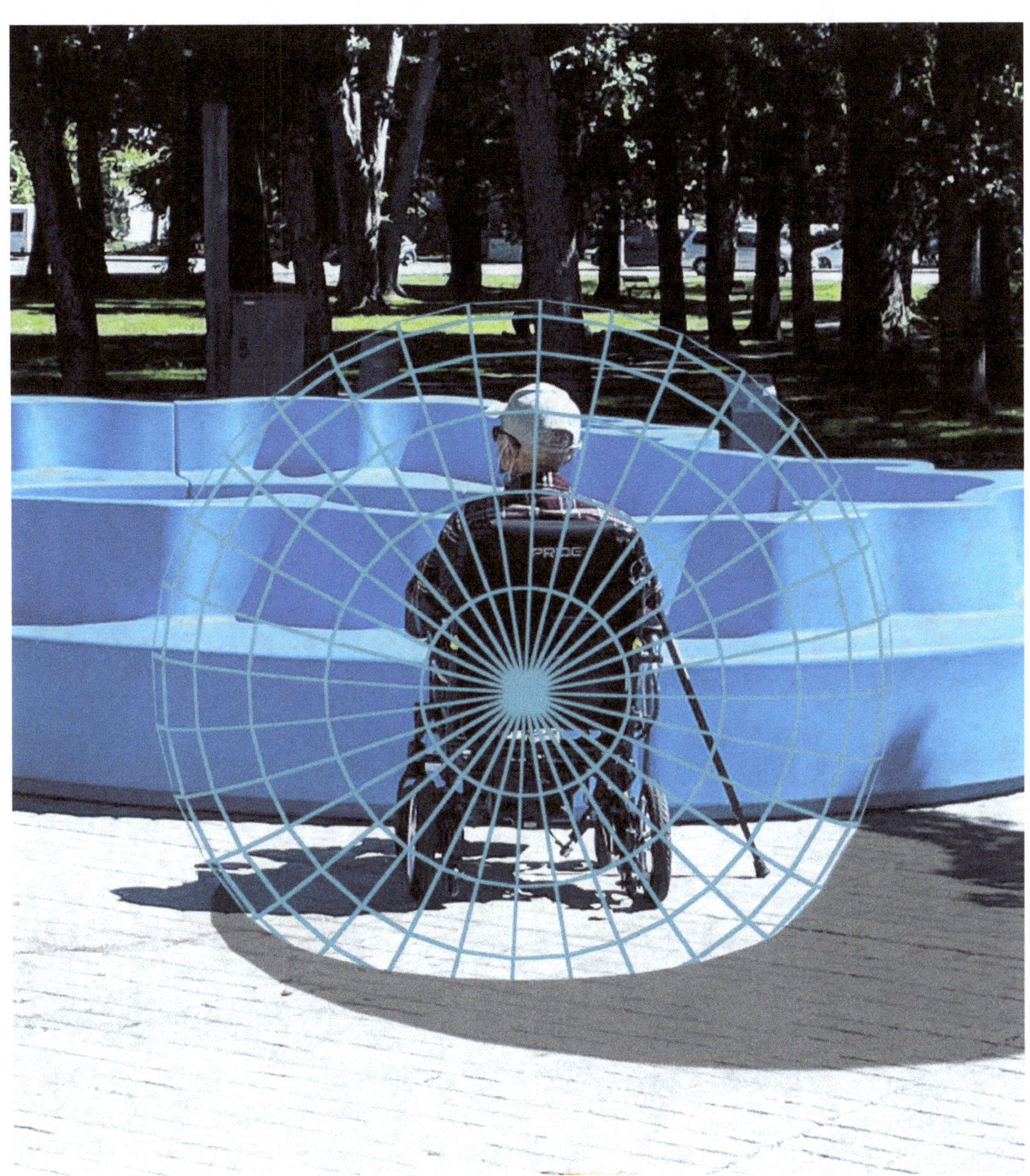

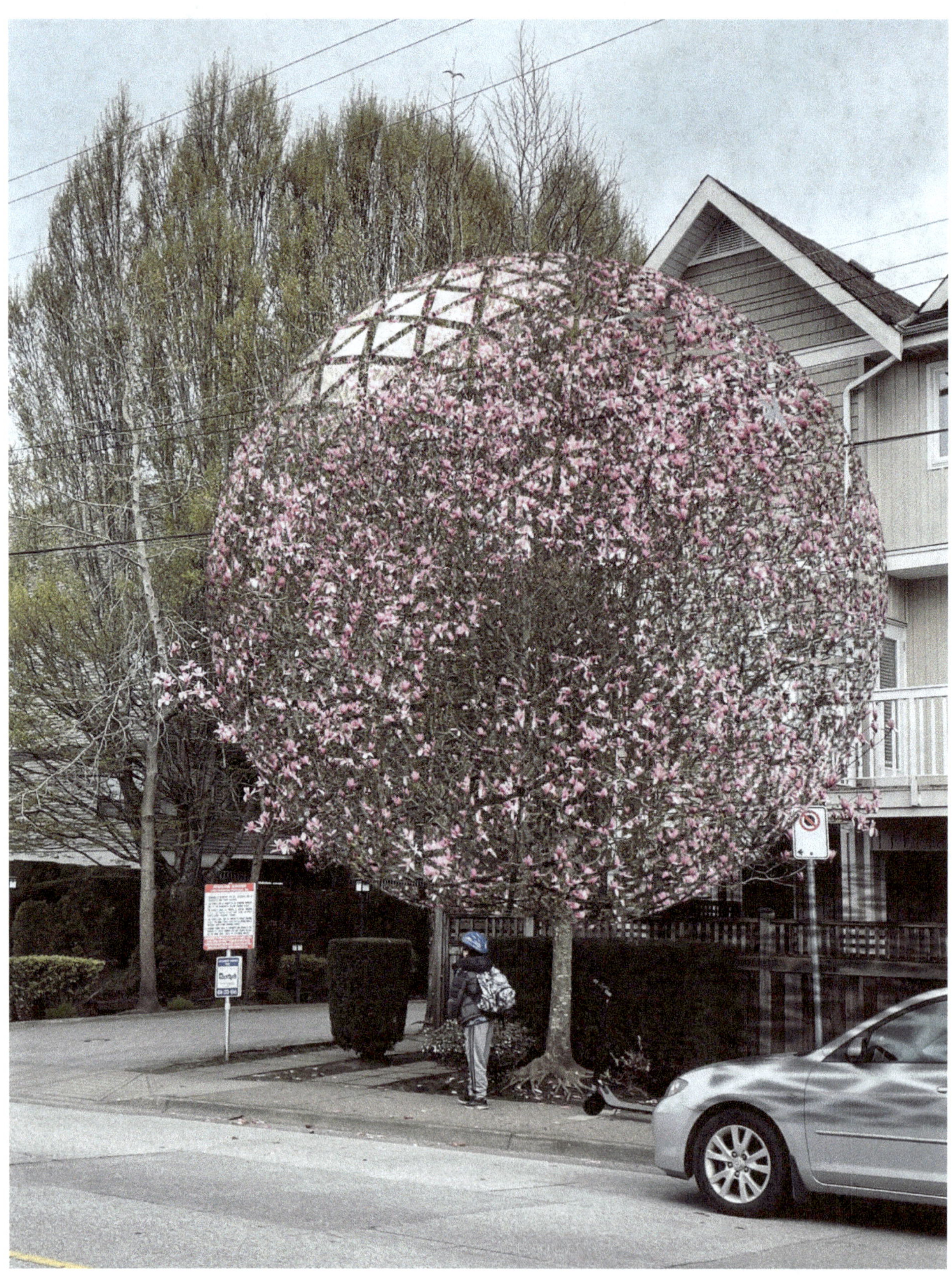

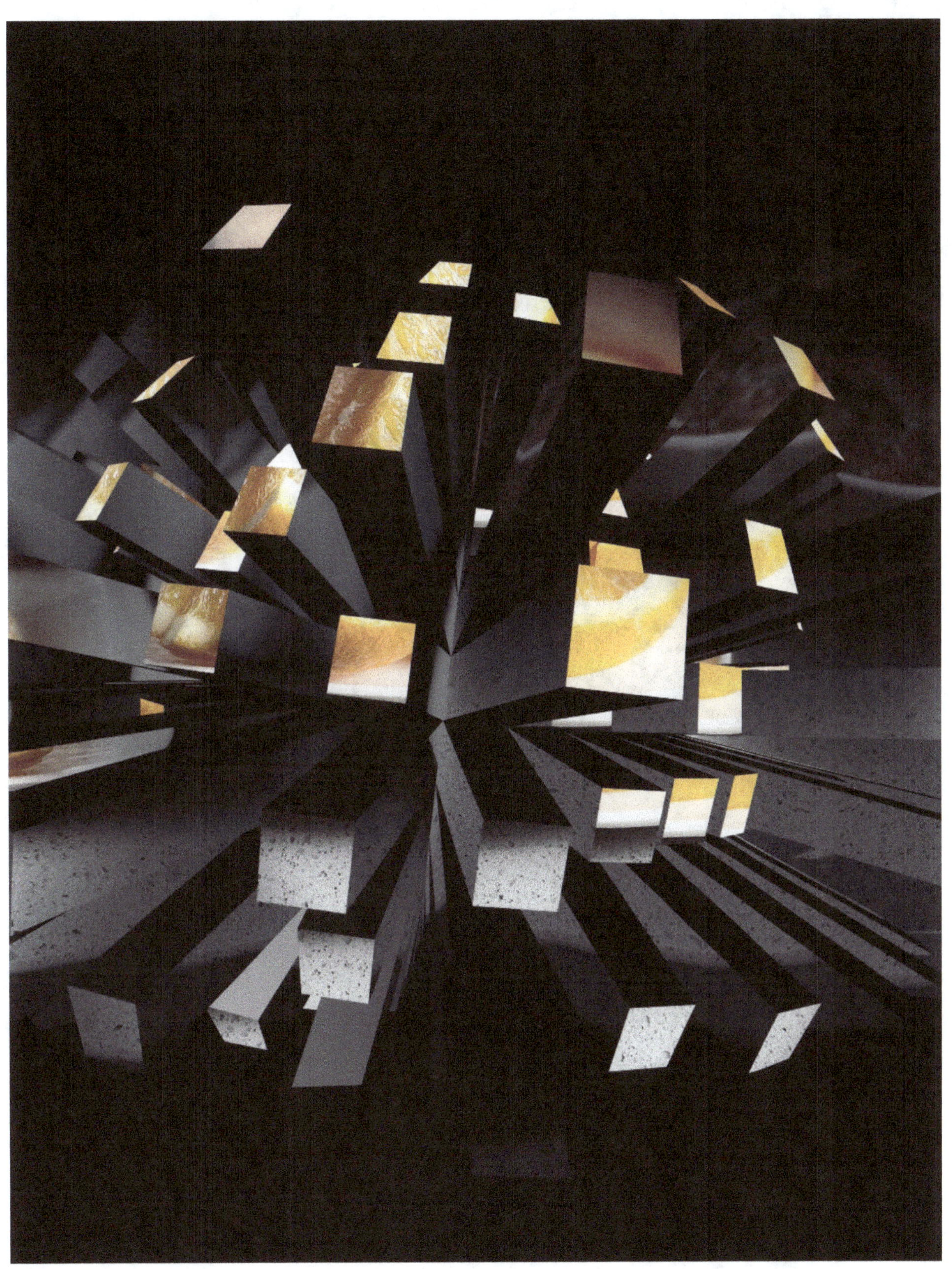

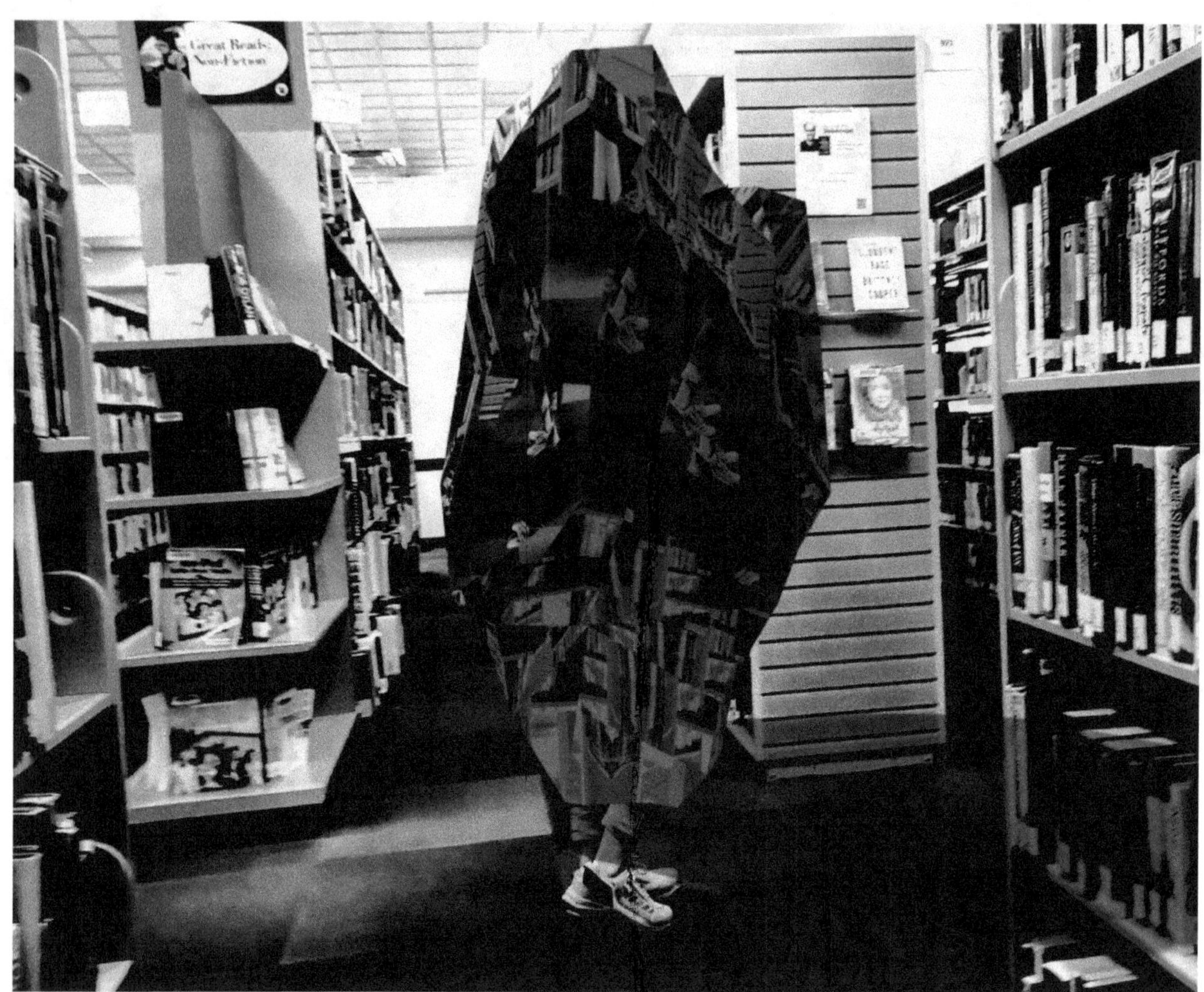

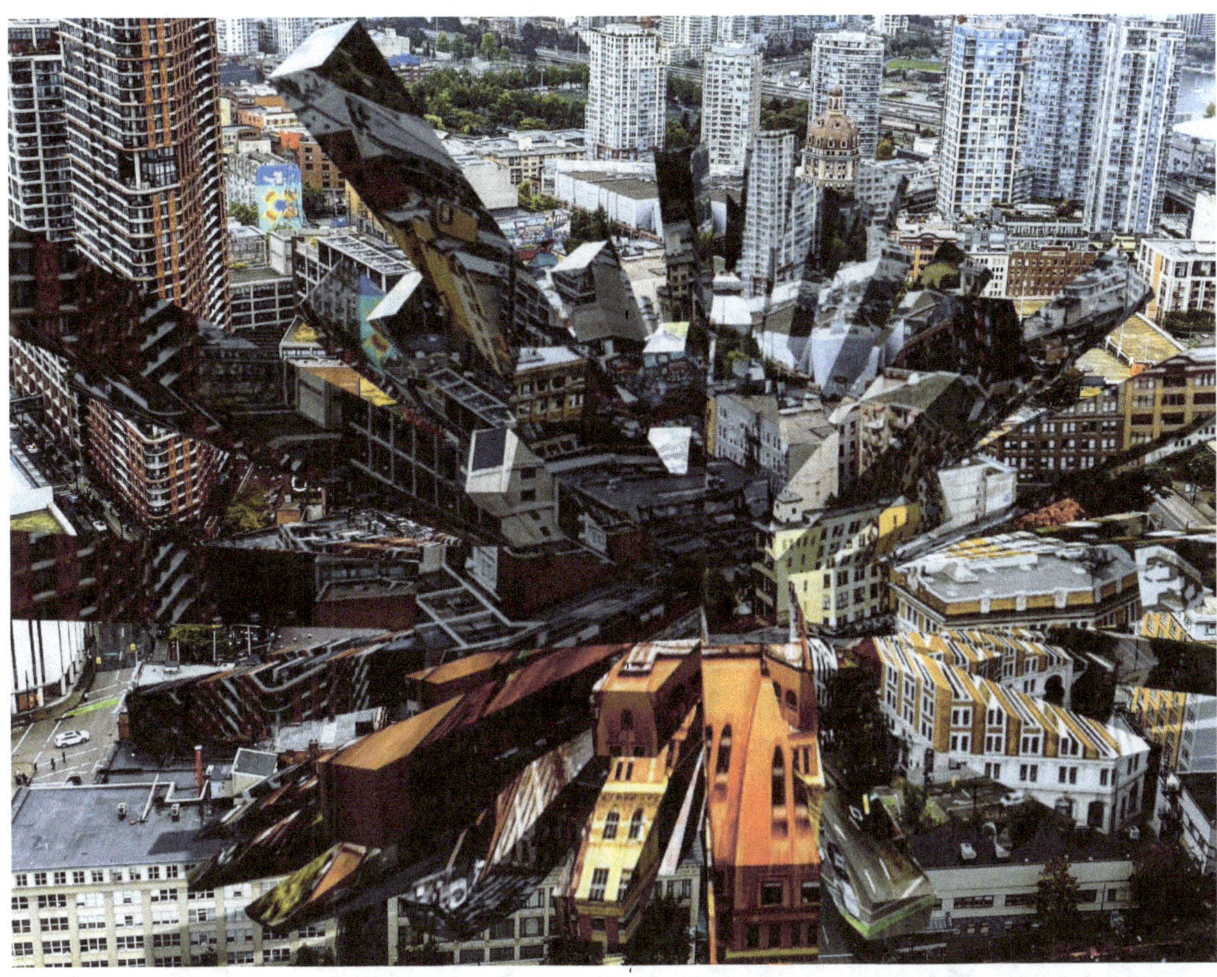

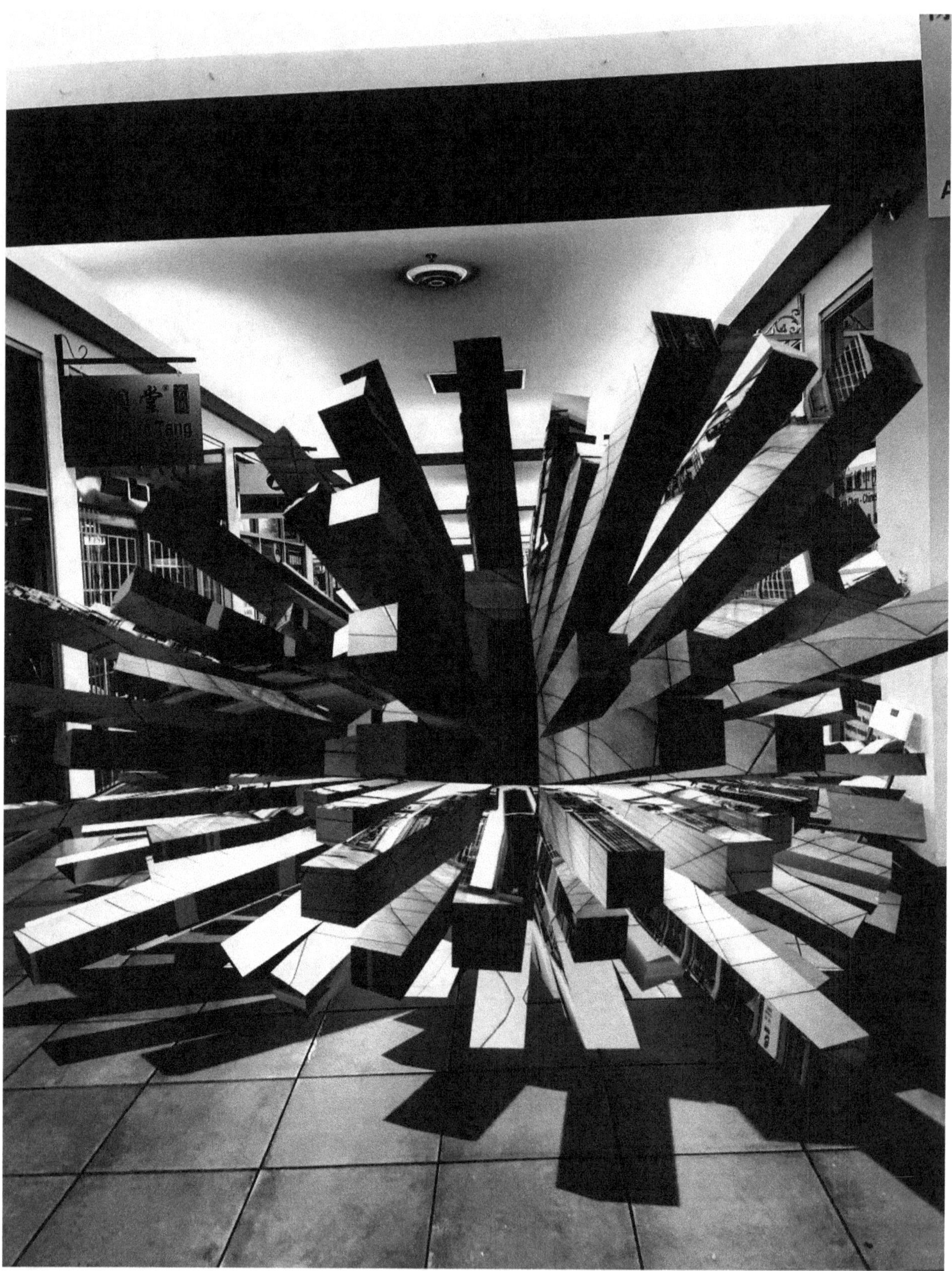

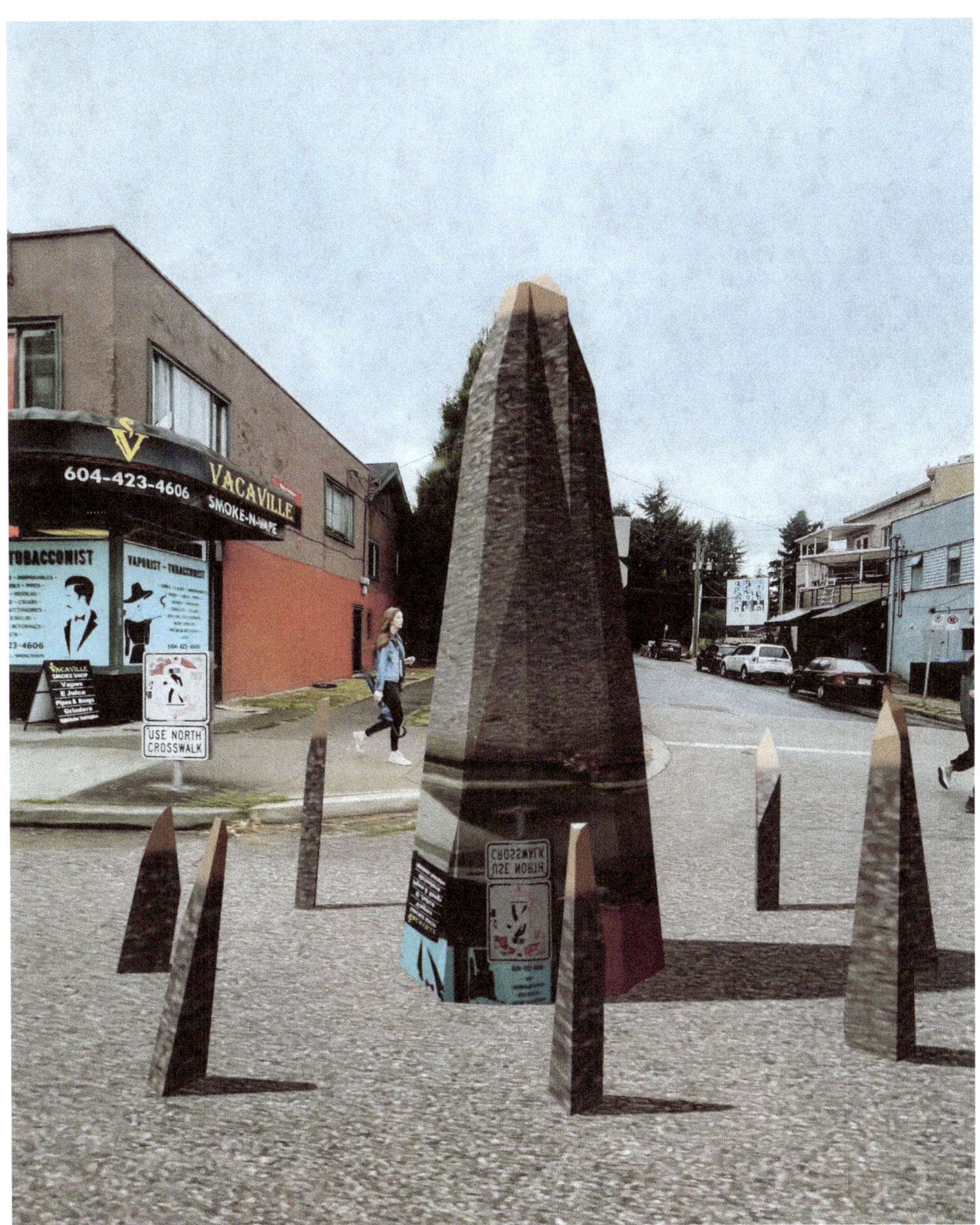
604-423-4606
VACAVILLE
SMOKE-N-VAPE
TOBACCONIST
VAPORIST - TOBACCONIST
VACAVILLE
SMOKE SHOP
Vapes
E Juice
Pipes & Bongs
Grinders
USE NORTH
CROSSWALK

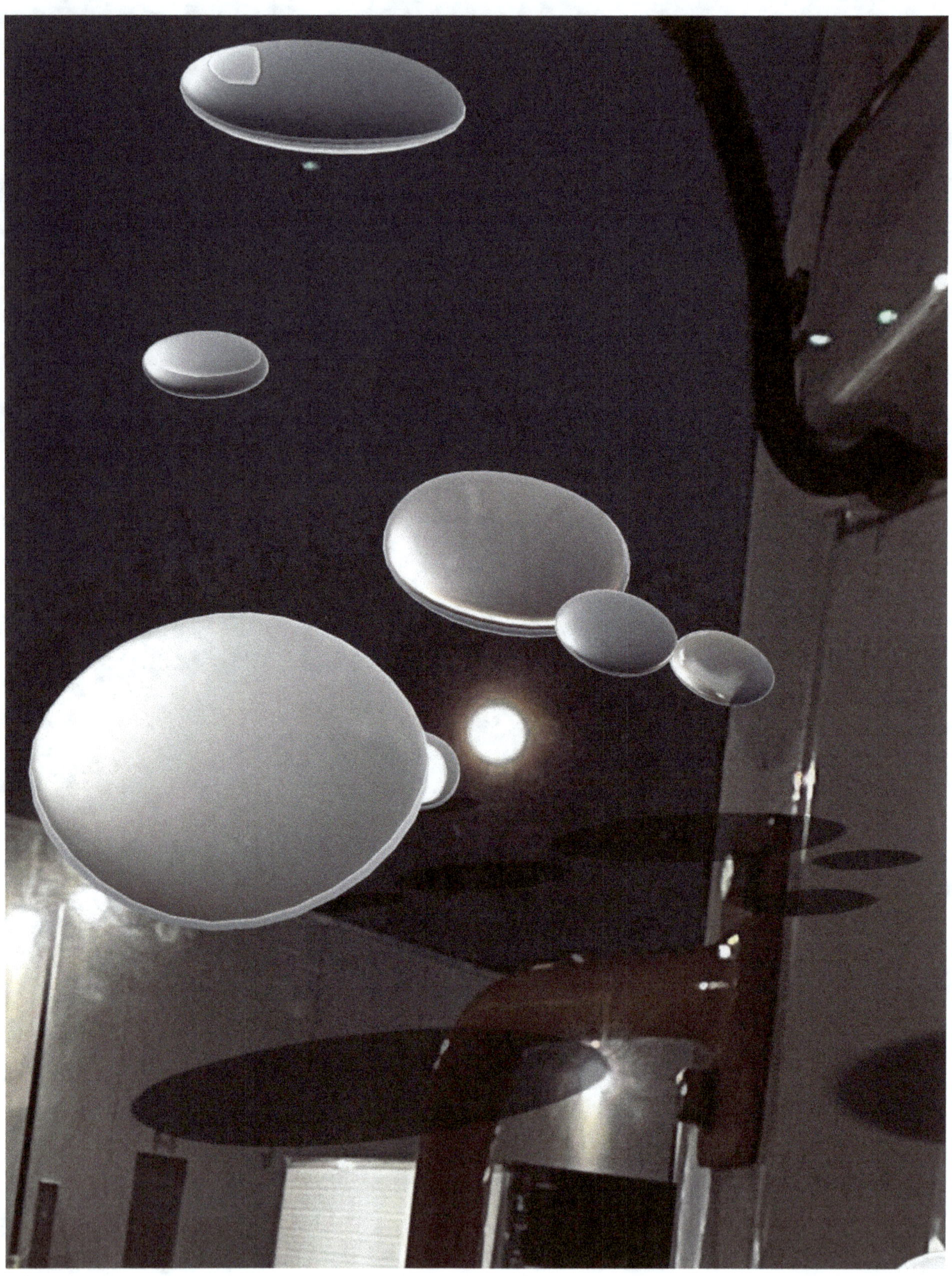

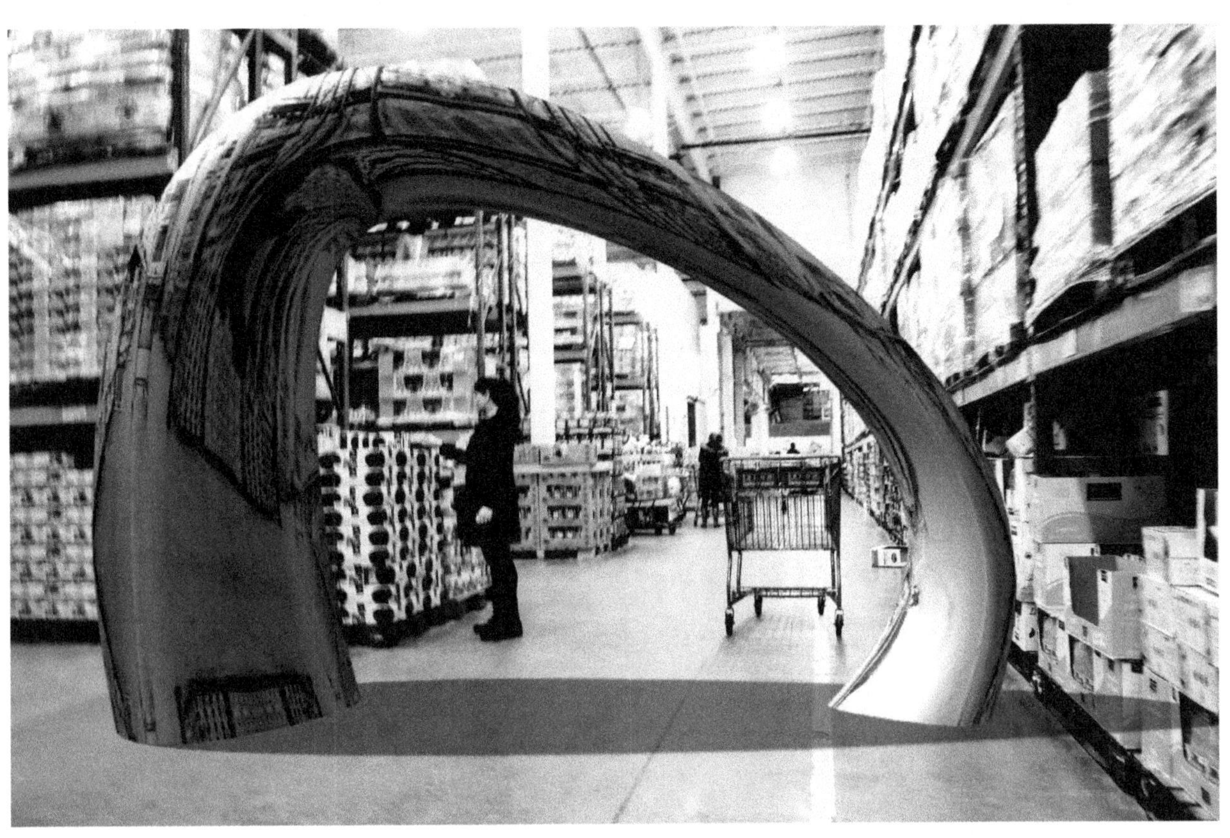

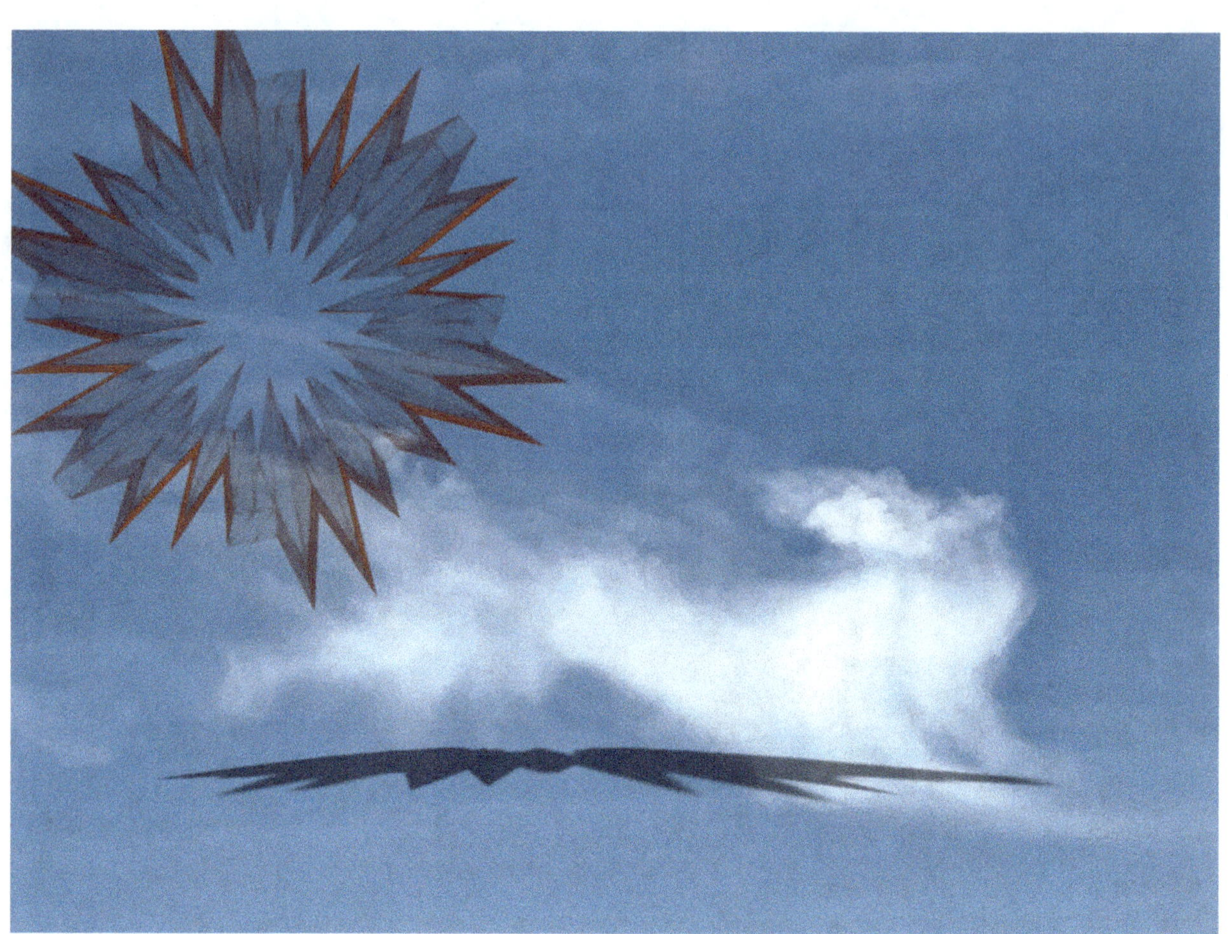

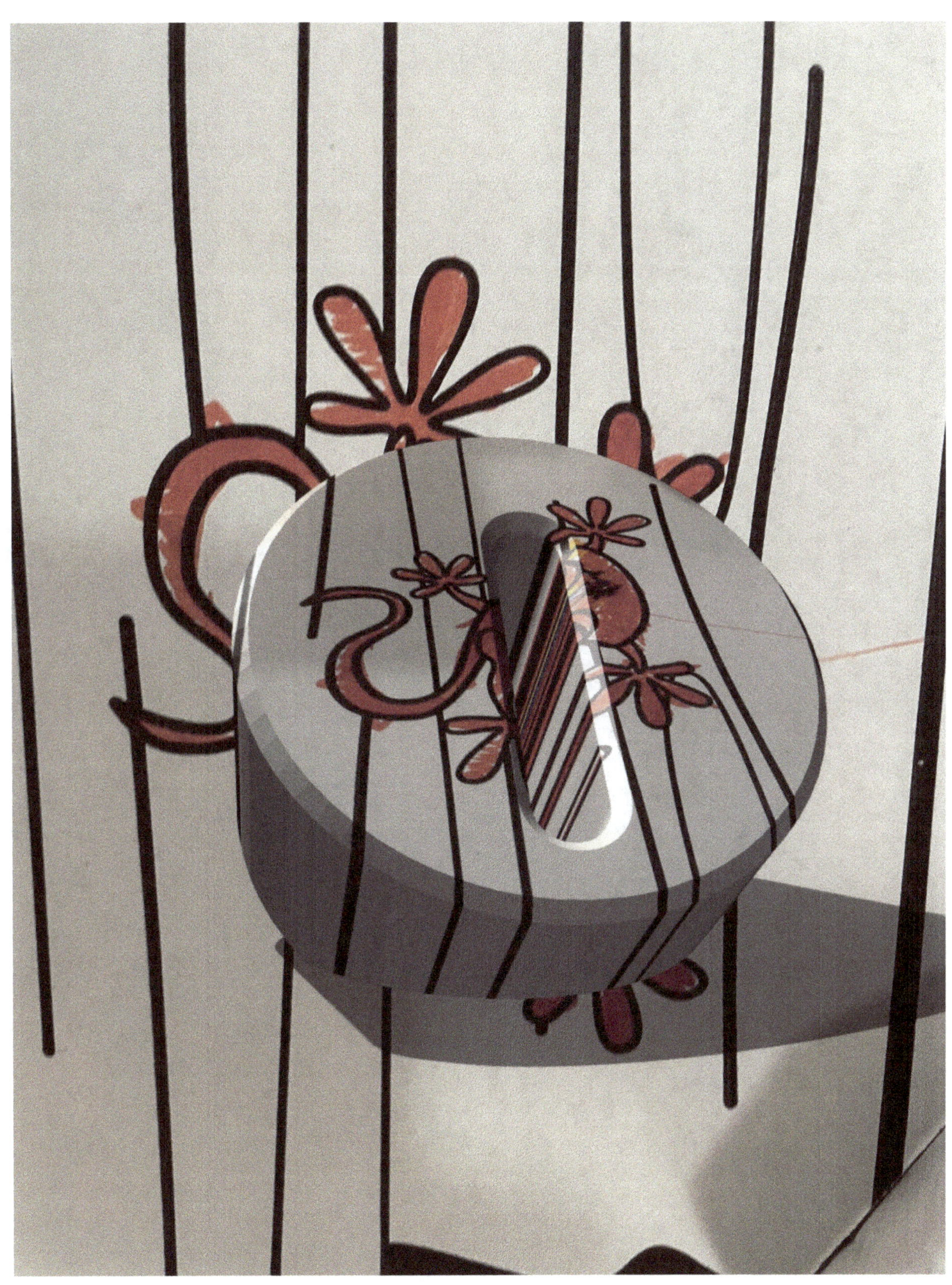

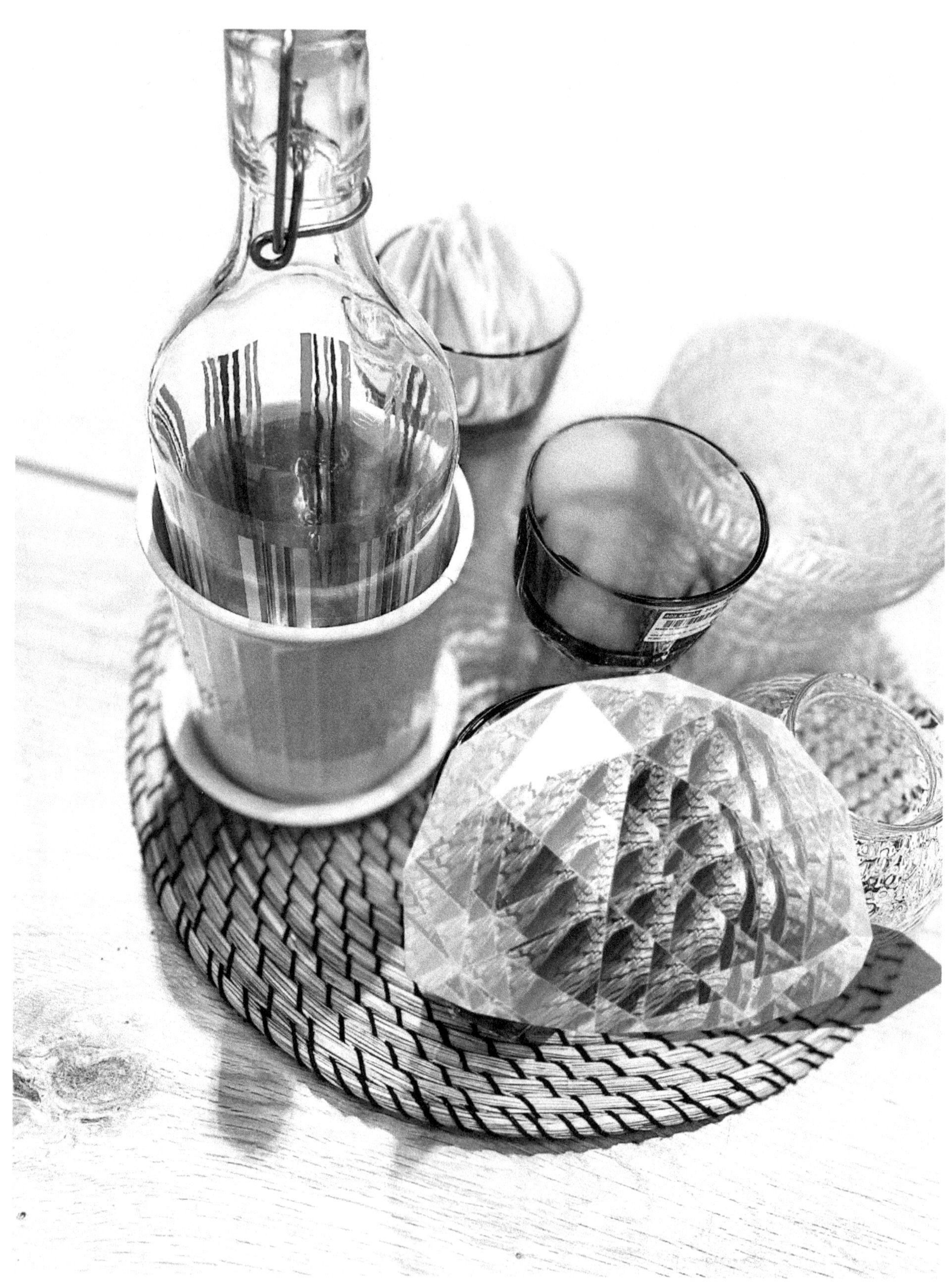

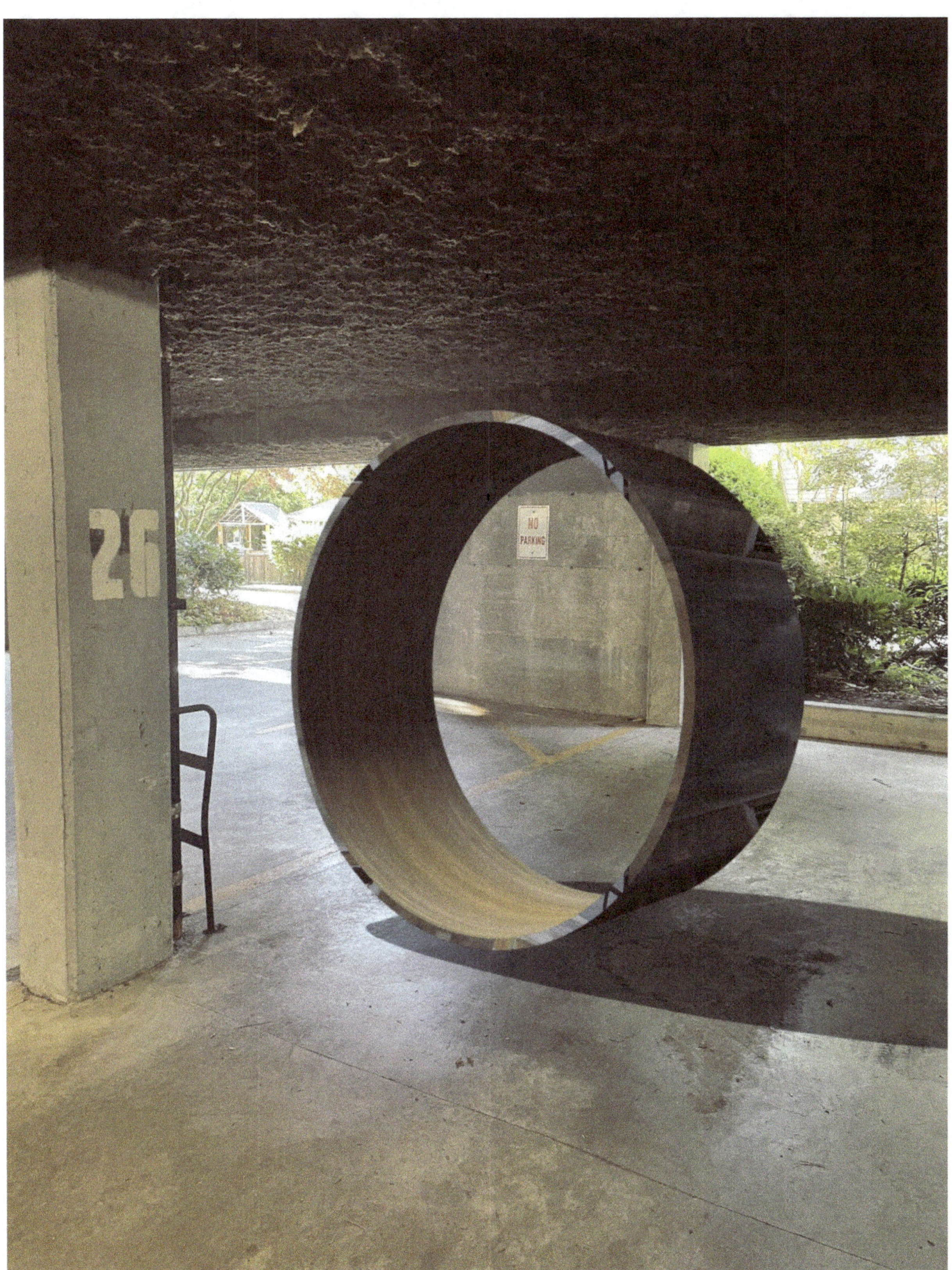
26
NO
PARKING

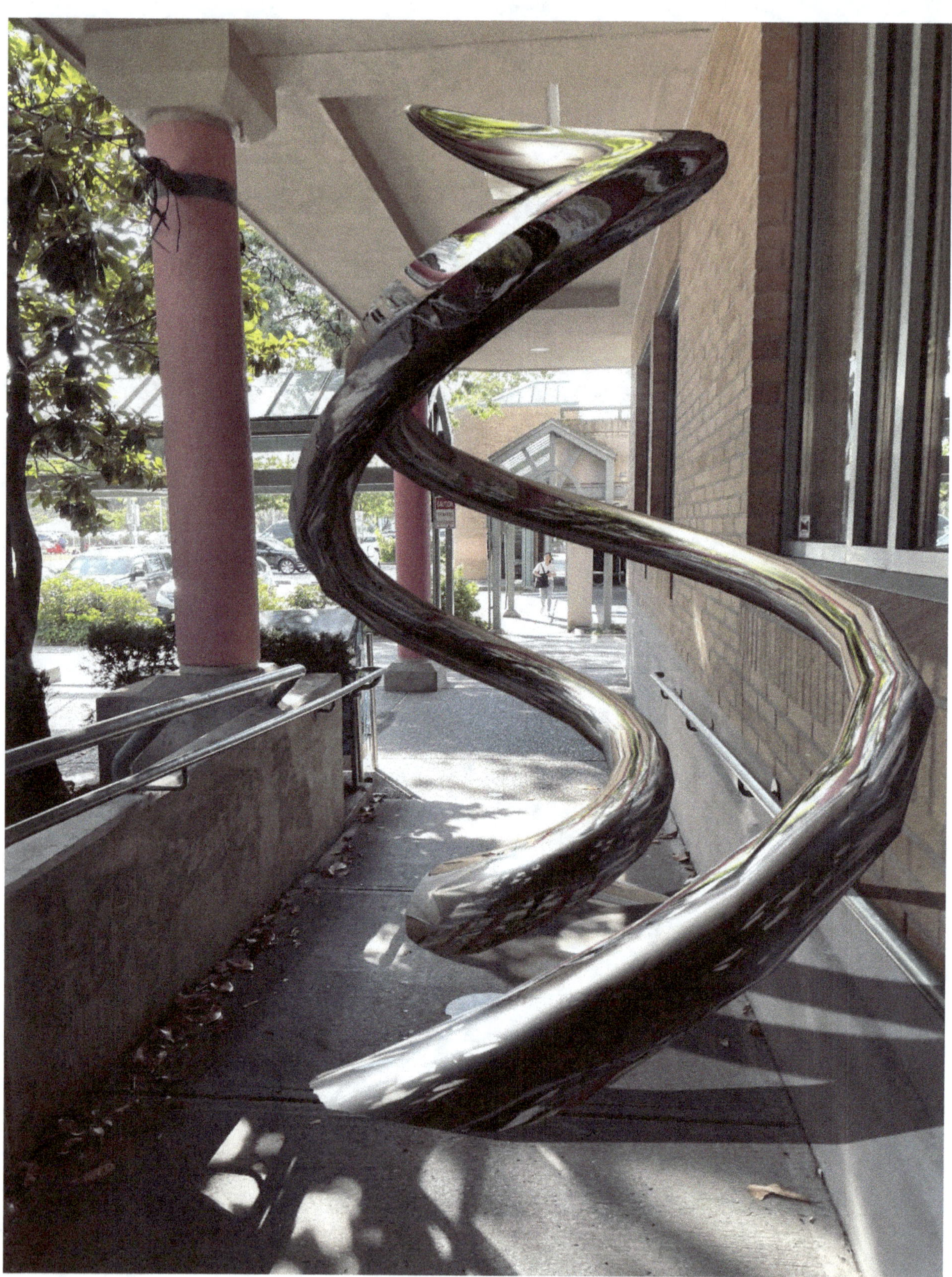

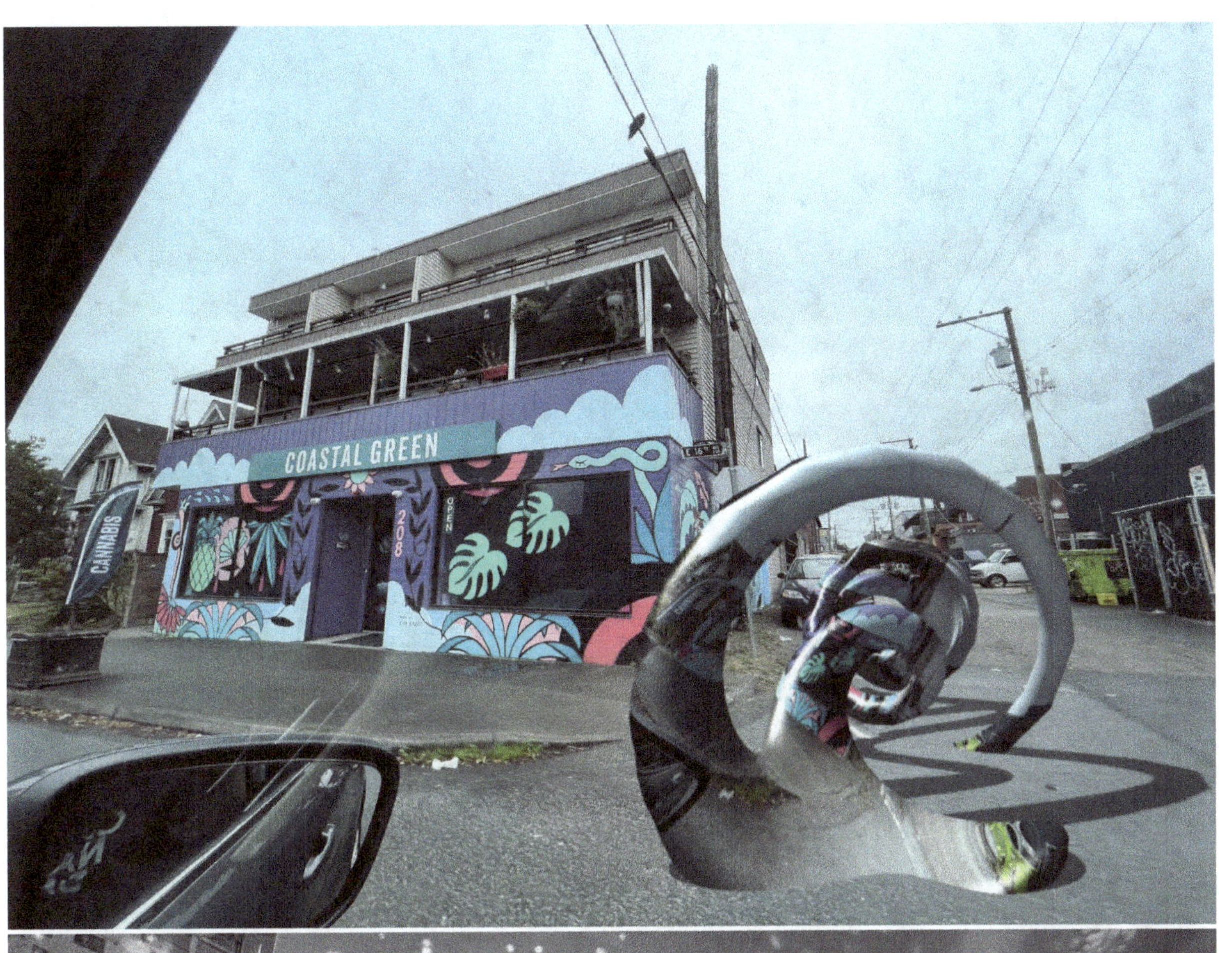

COASTAL GREEN
CANNABIS
OPEN
208

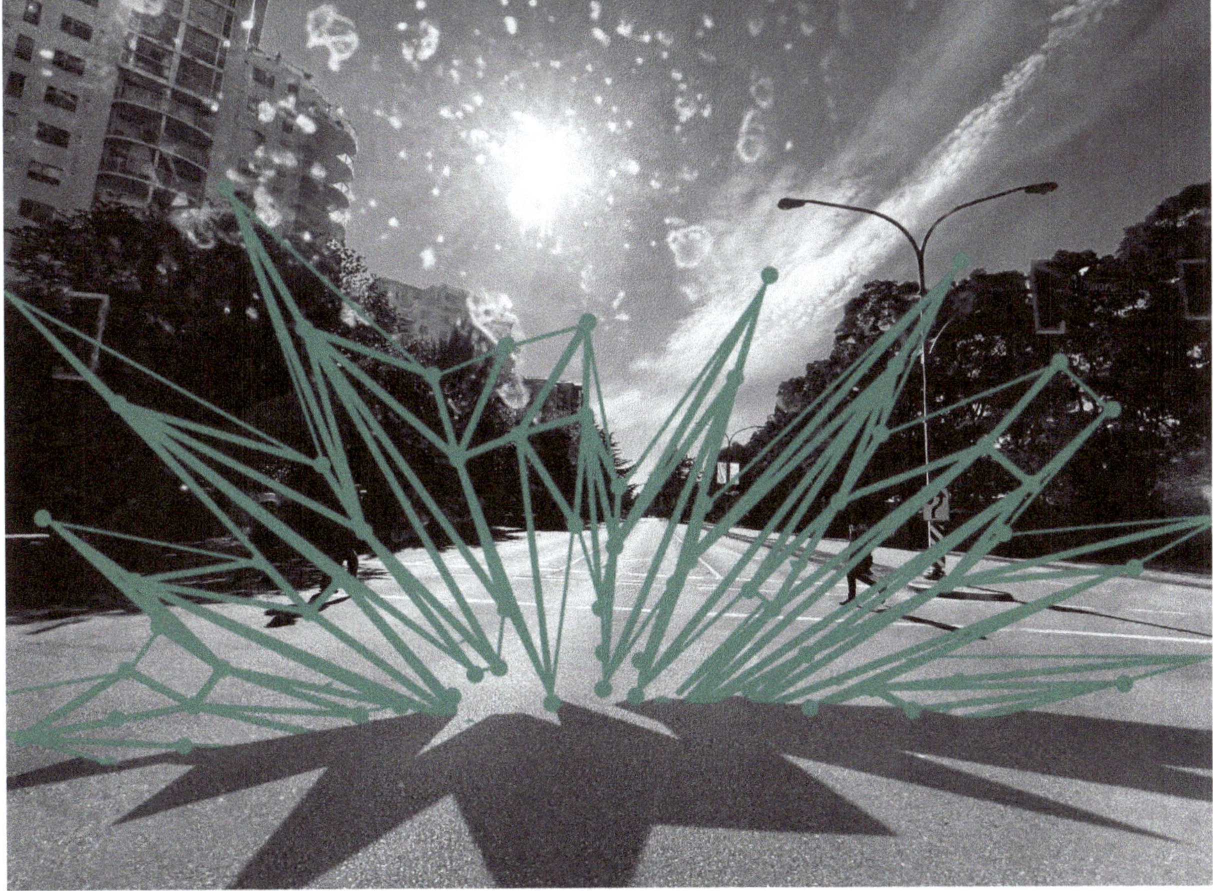

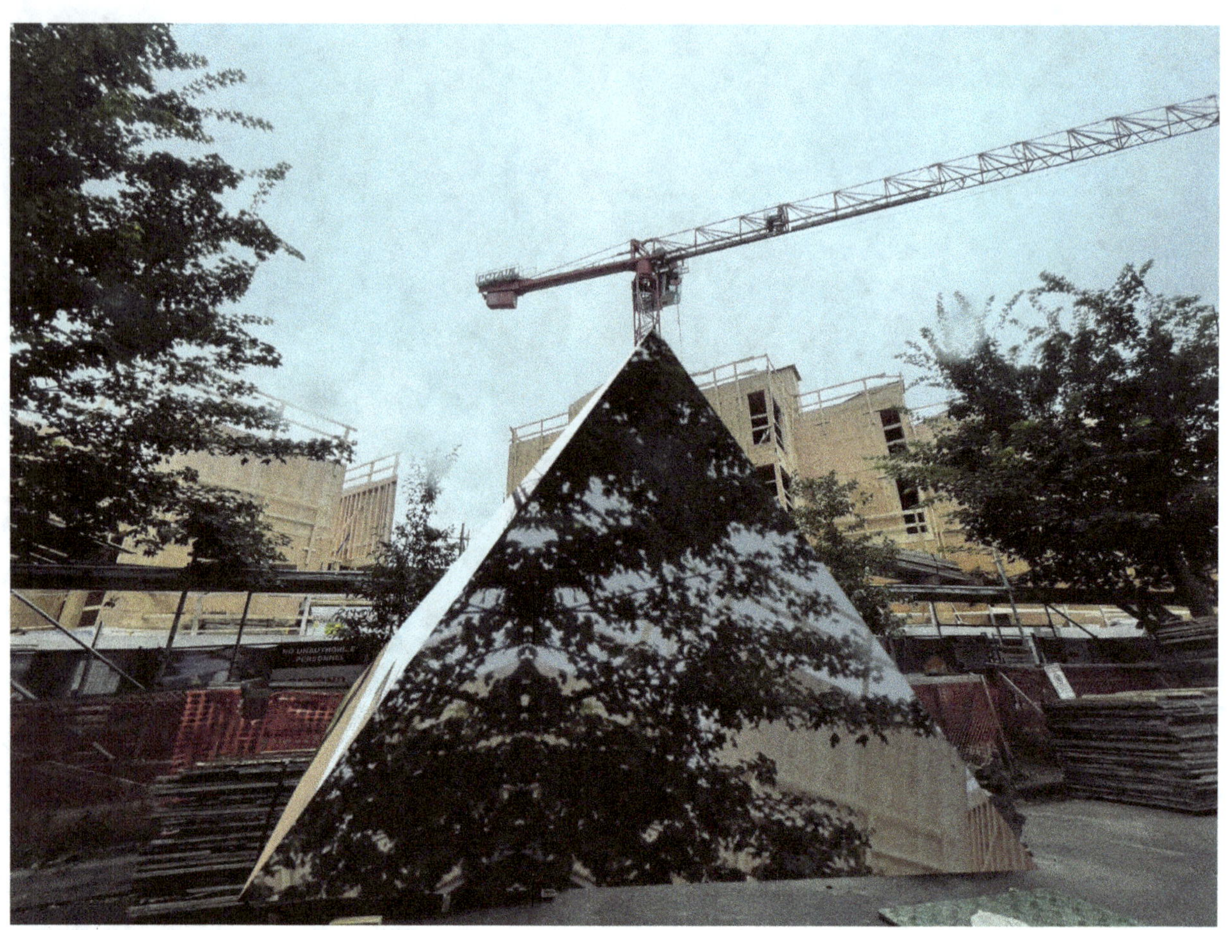

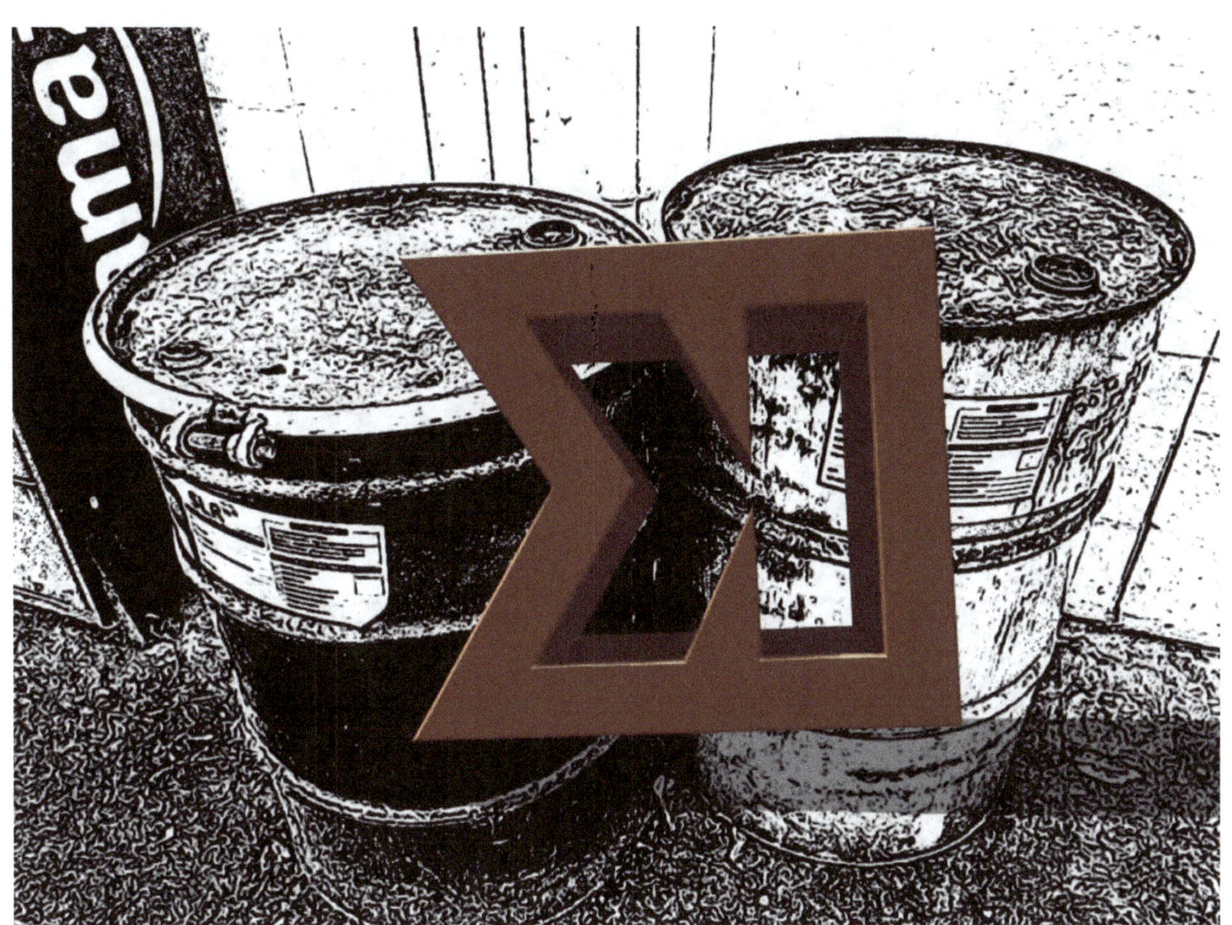

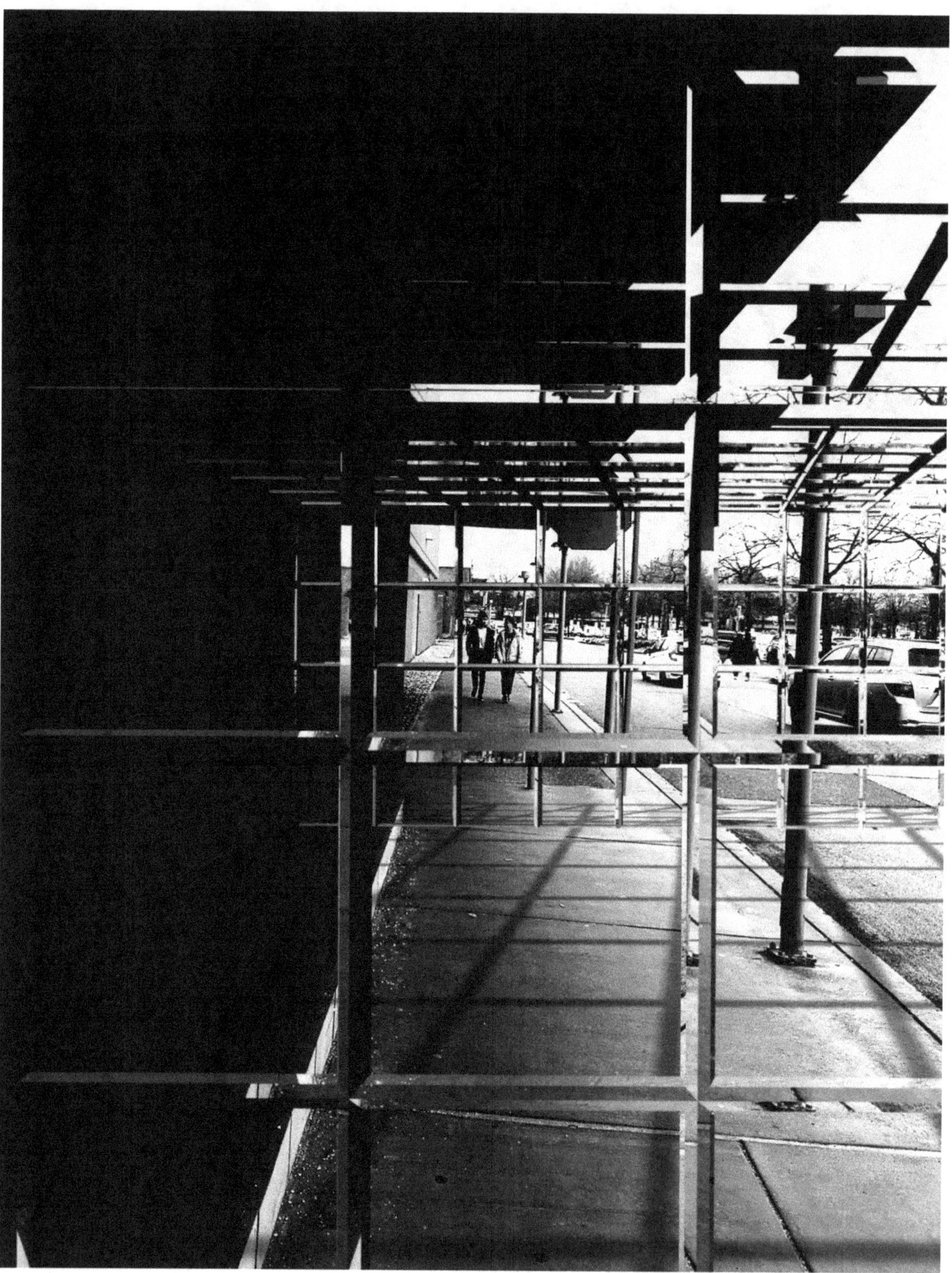

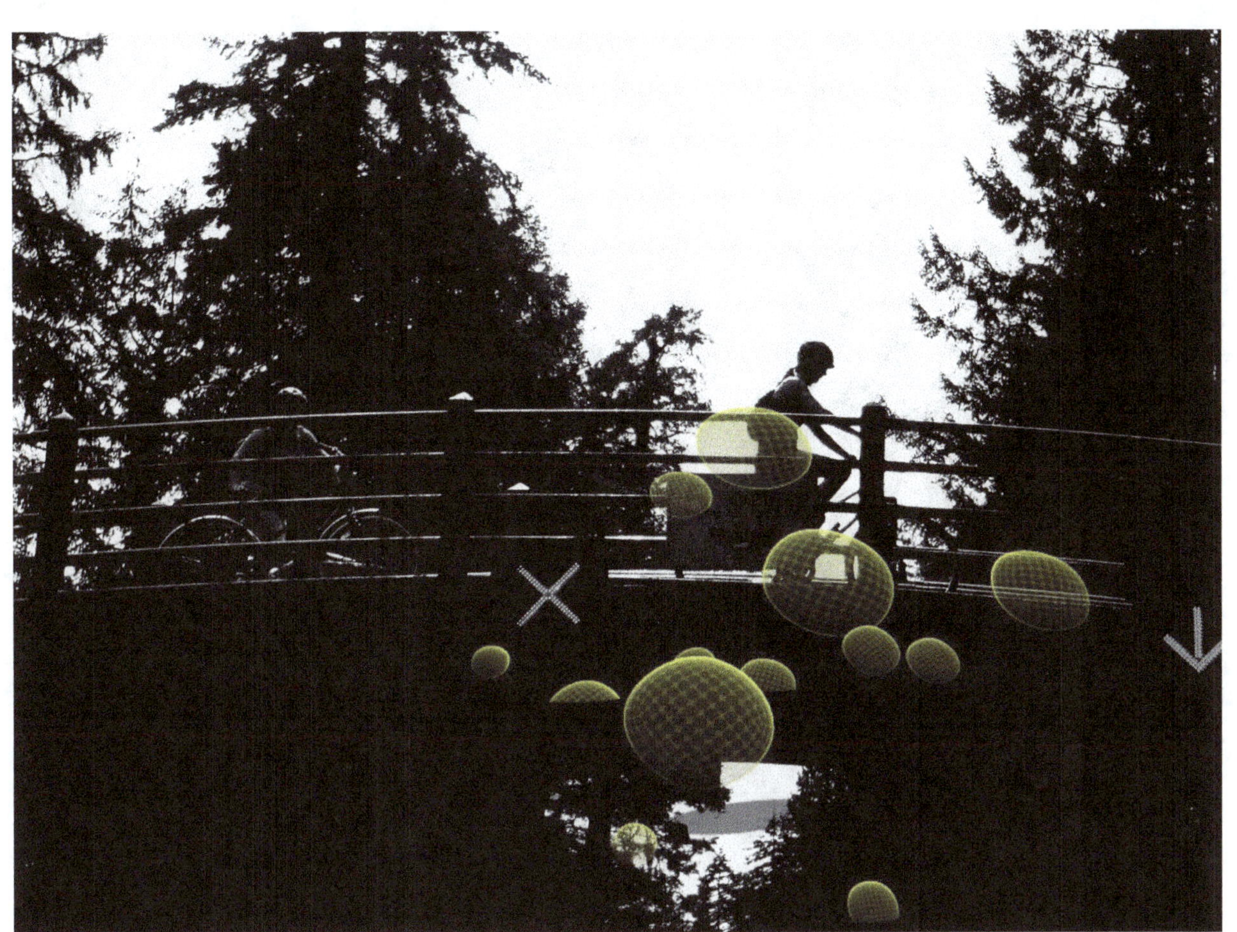

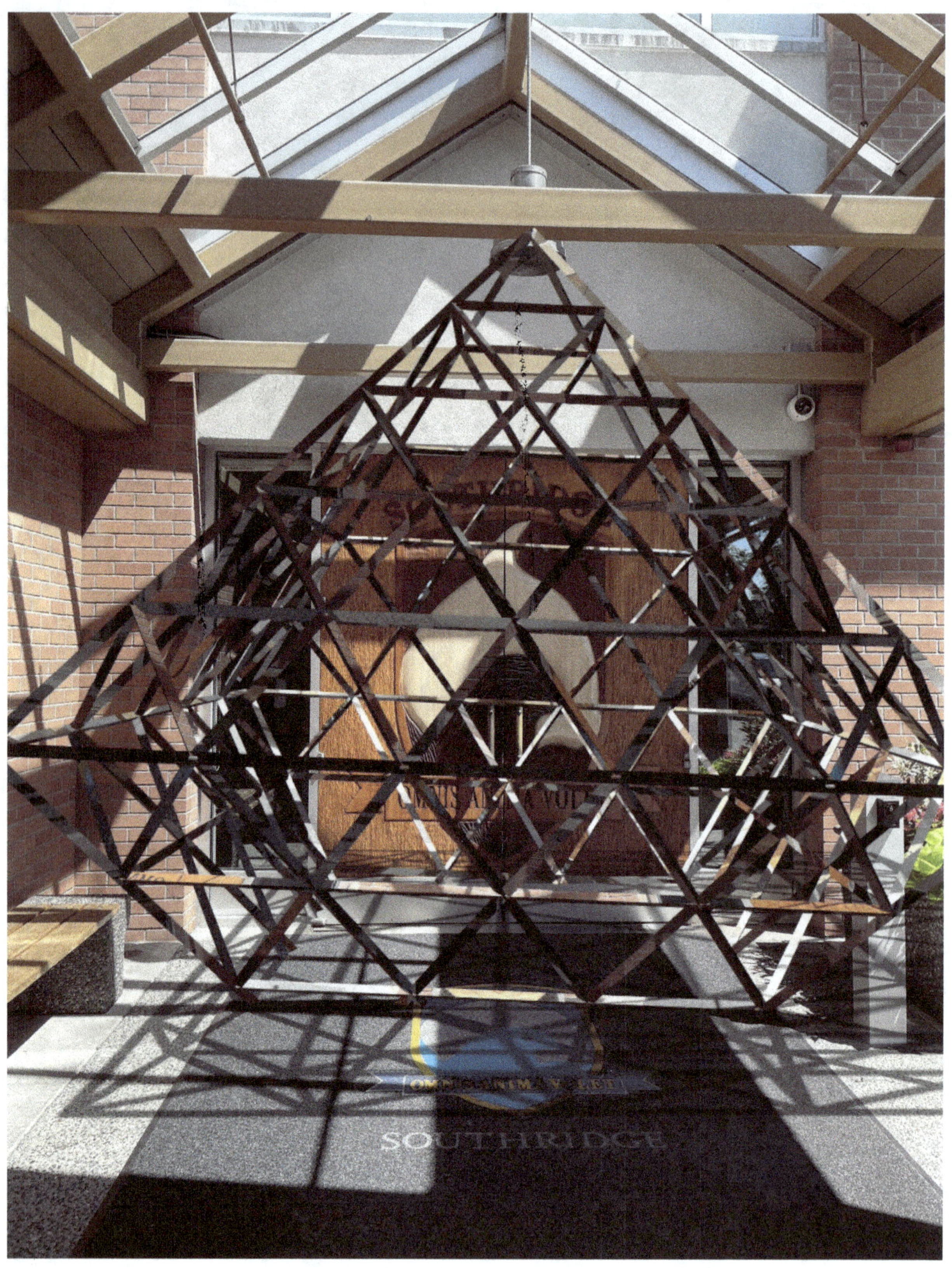
SOUTHRIDGE

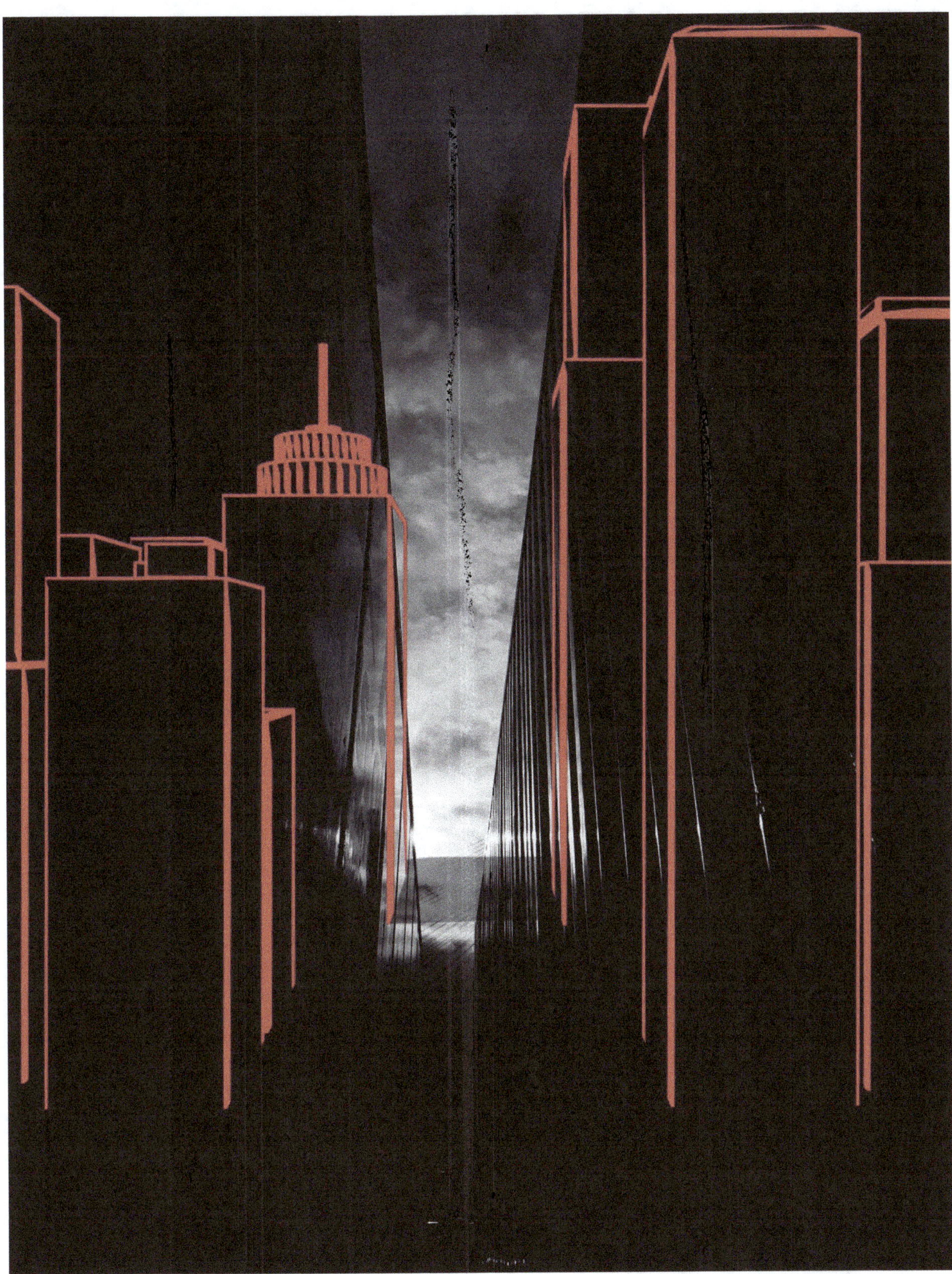

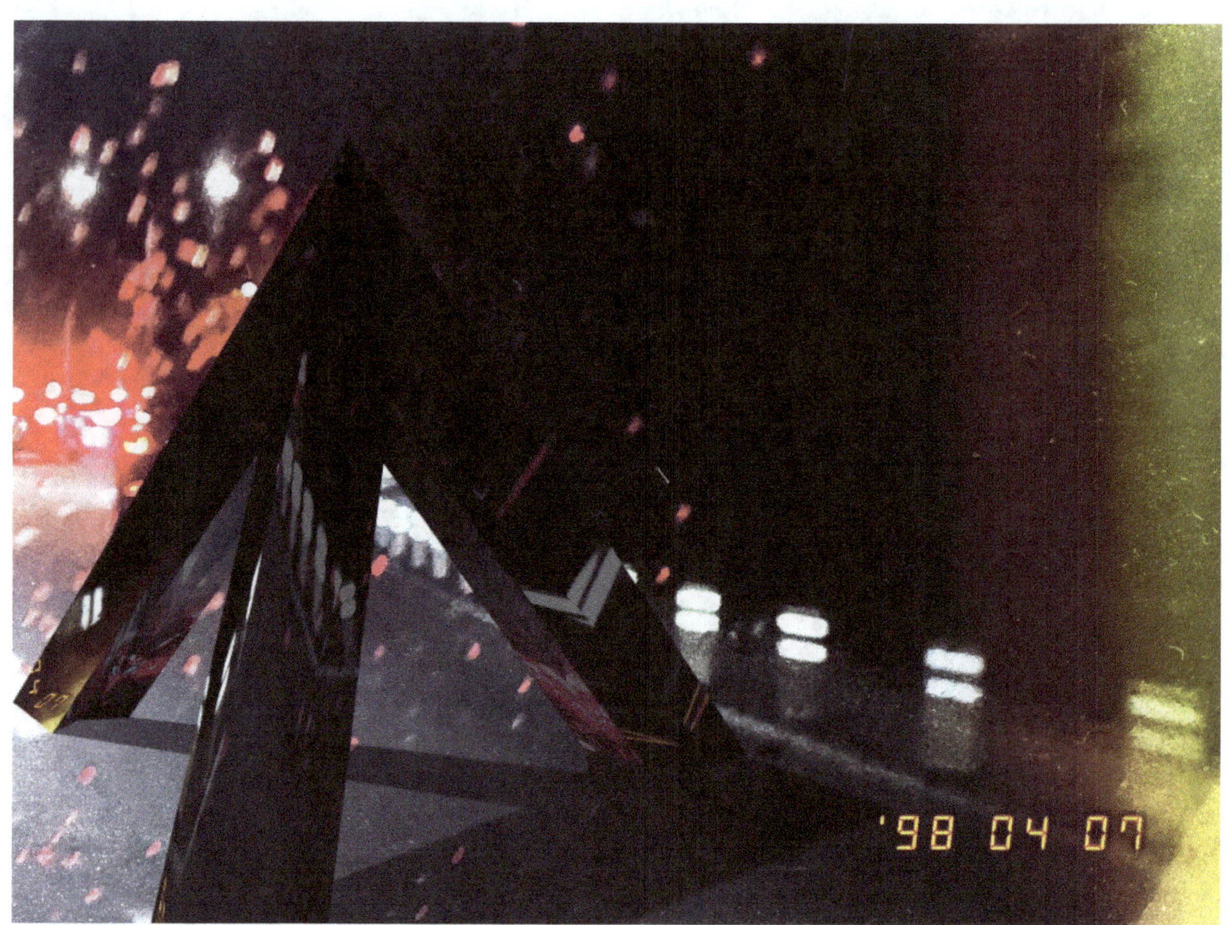
'98 04 07

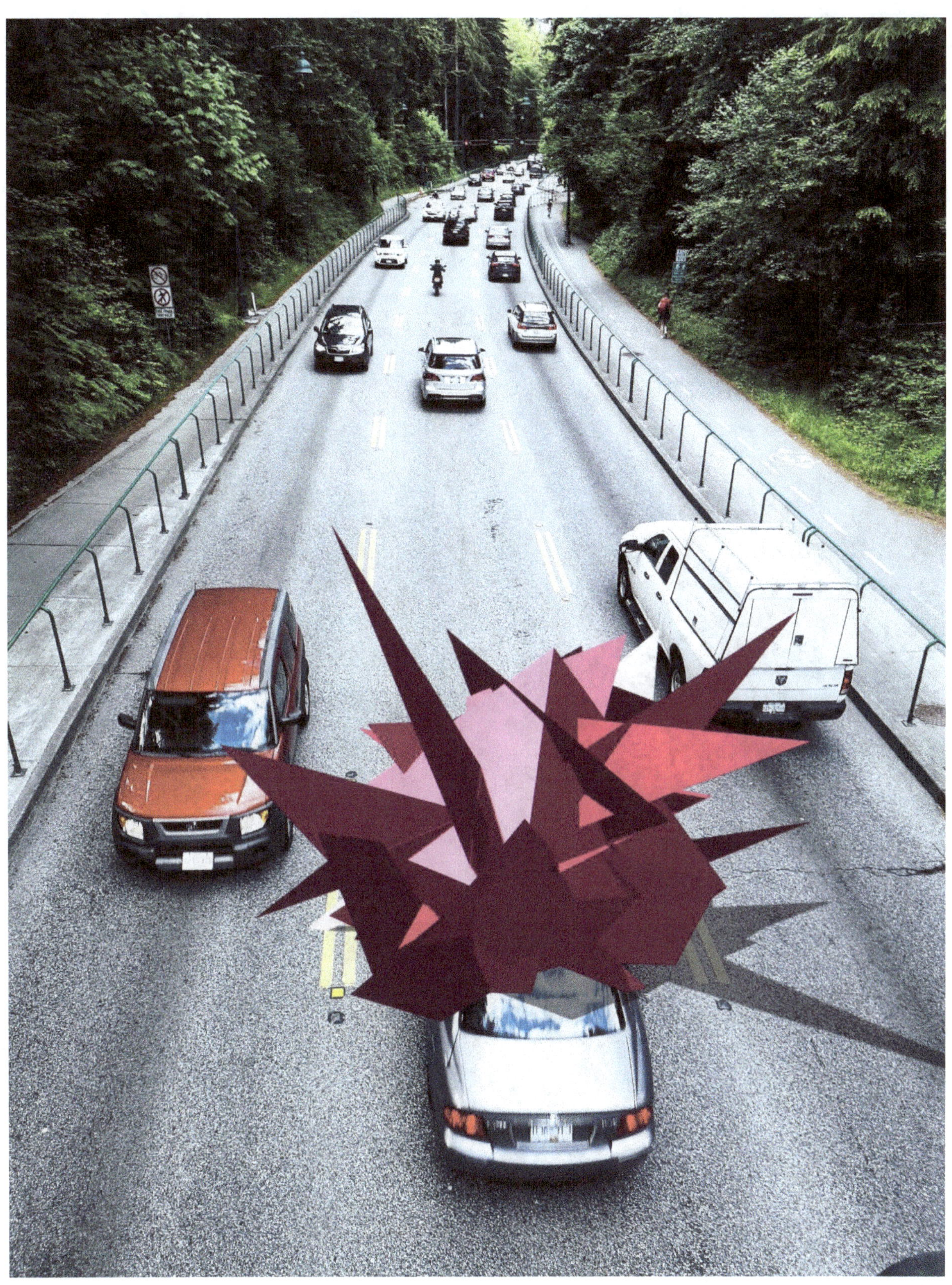

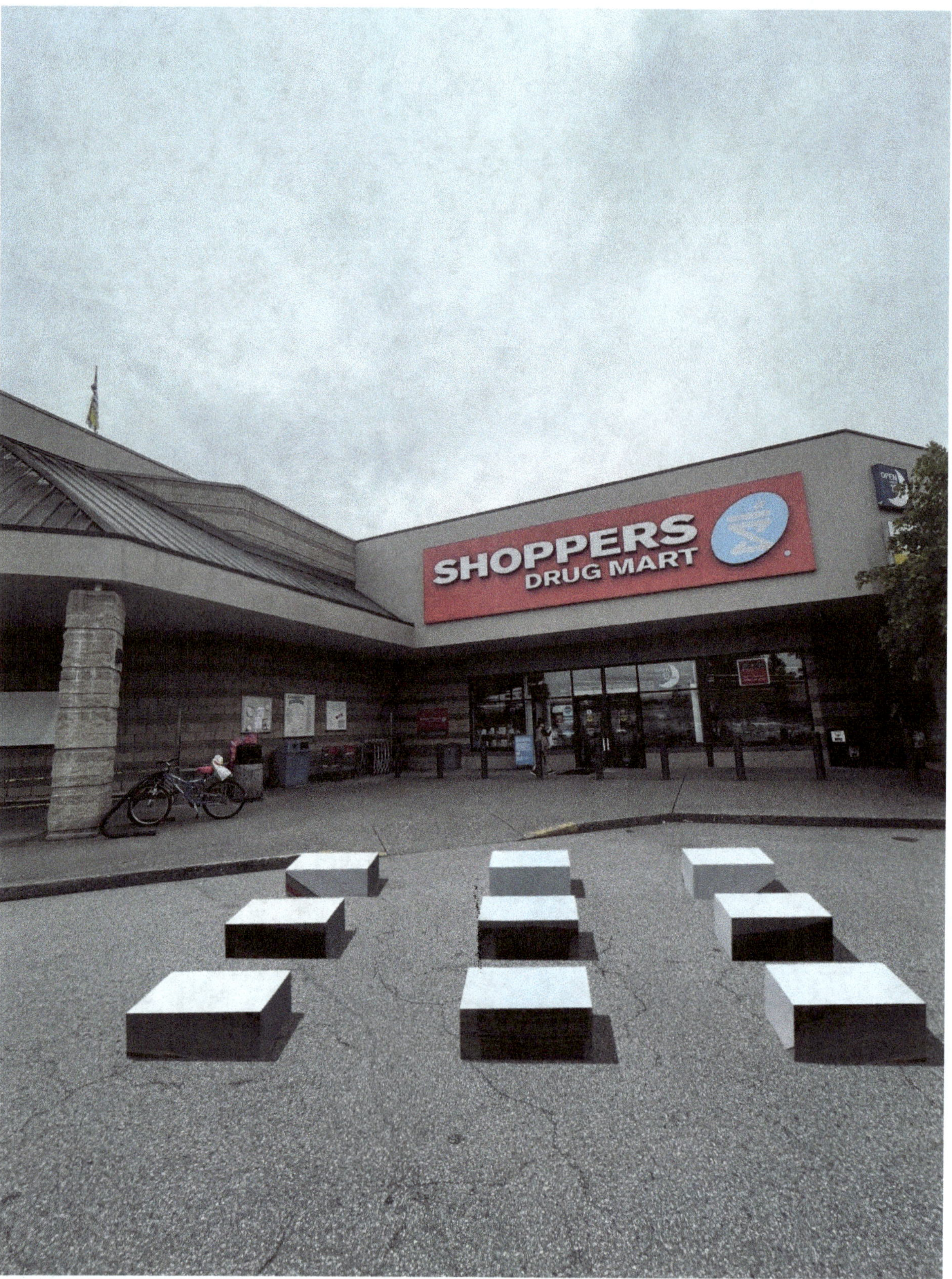

SHOPPERS
DRUG MART

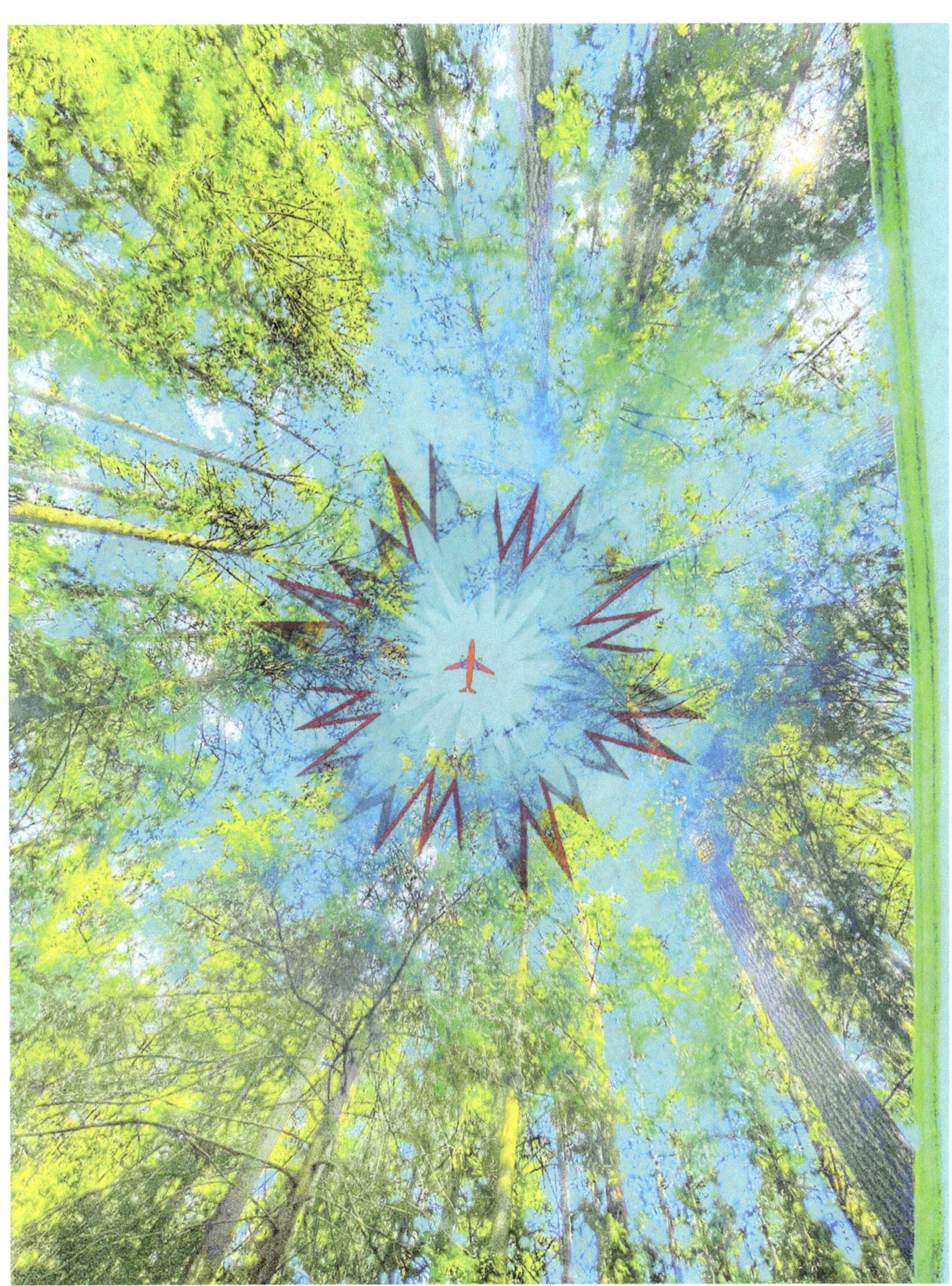

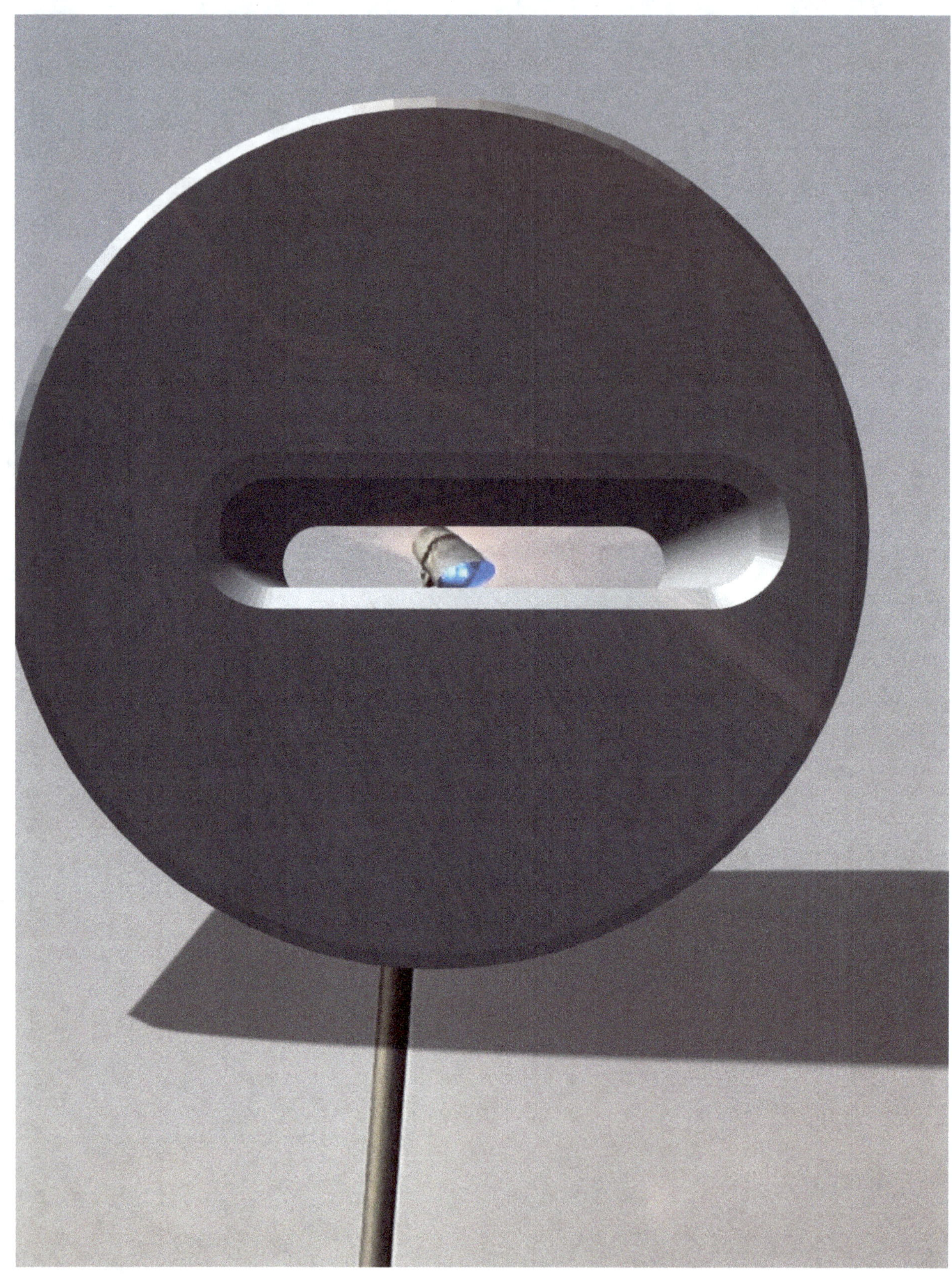

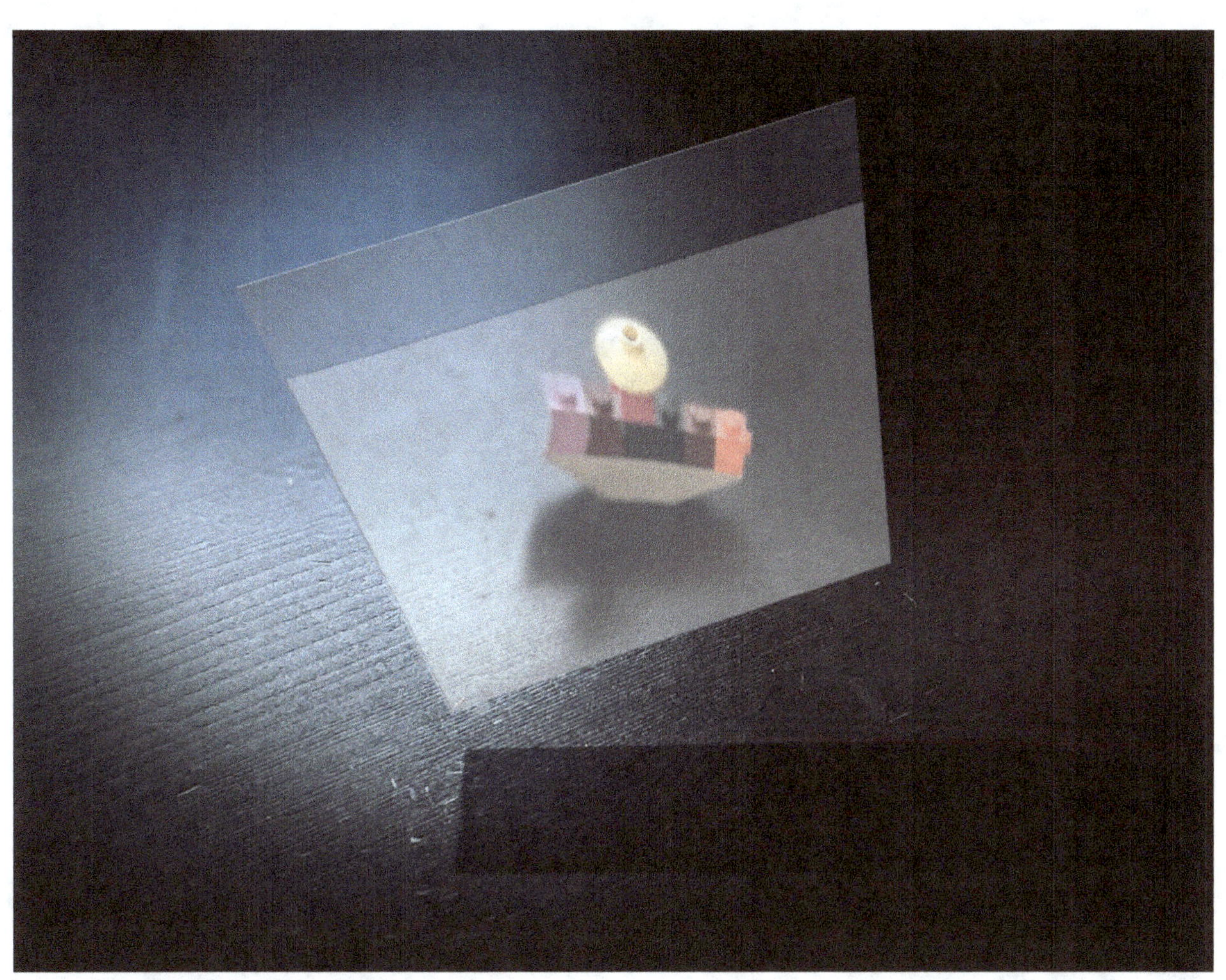

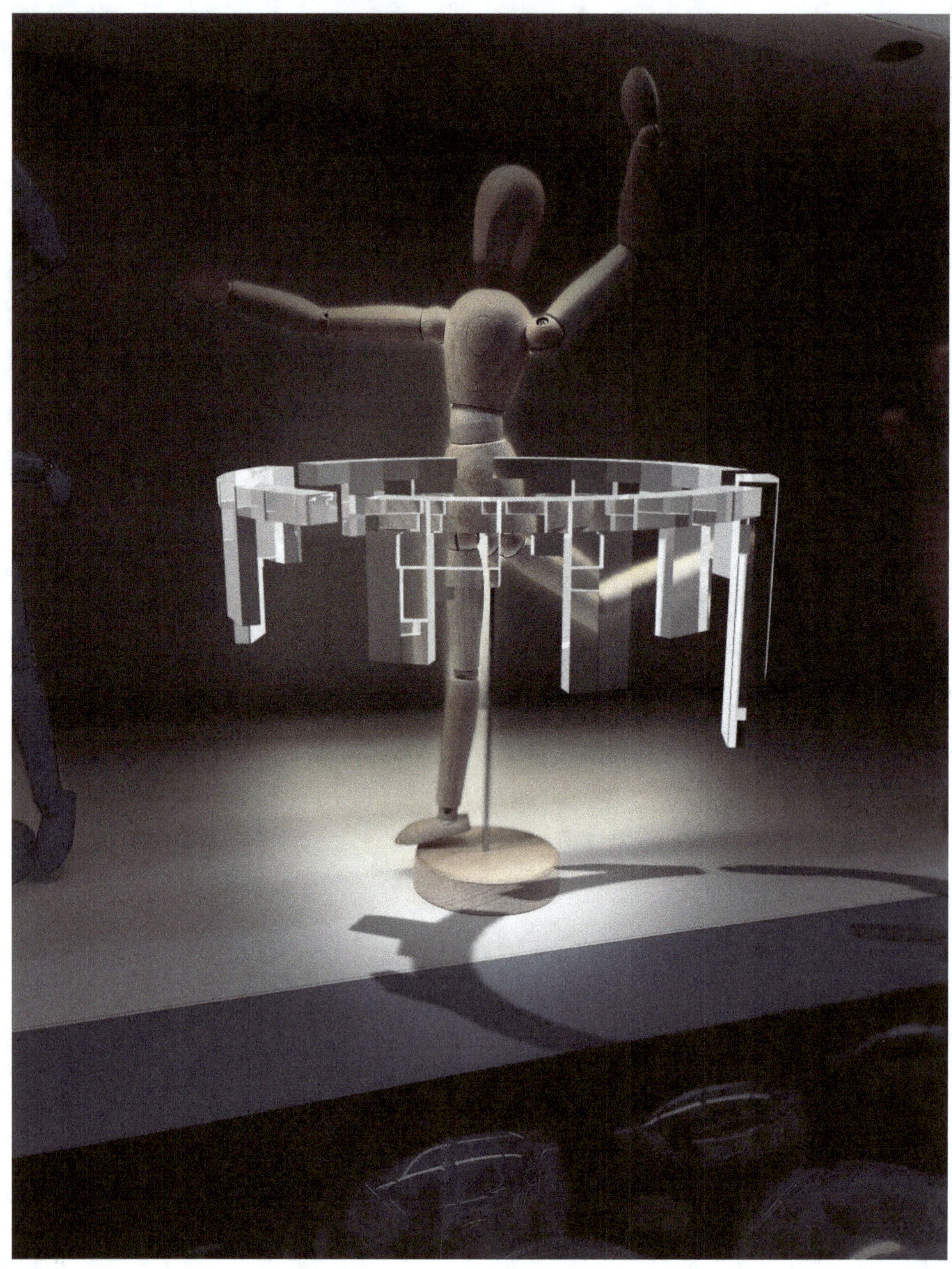

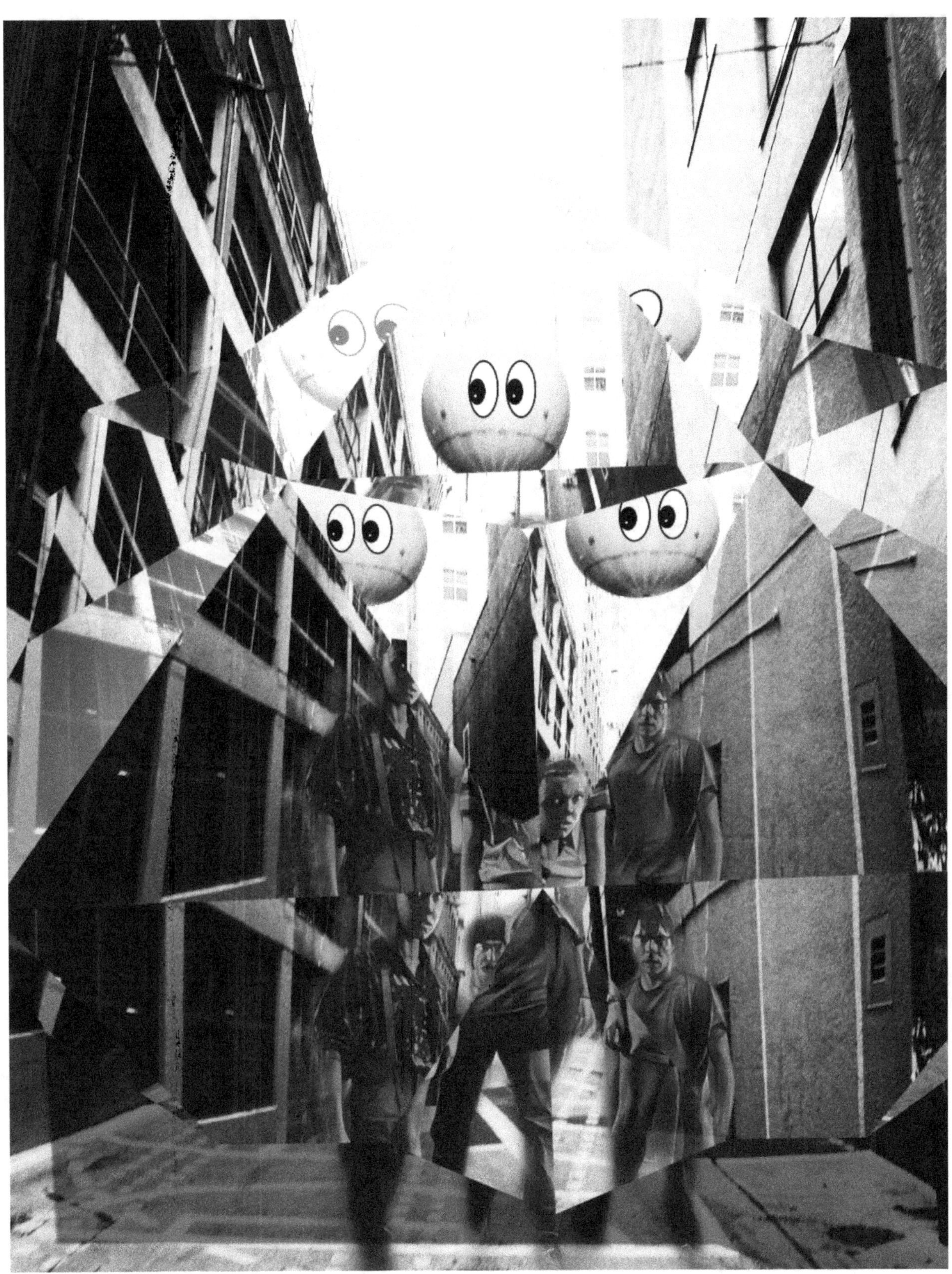

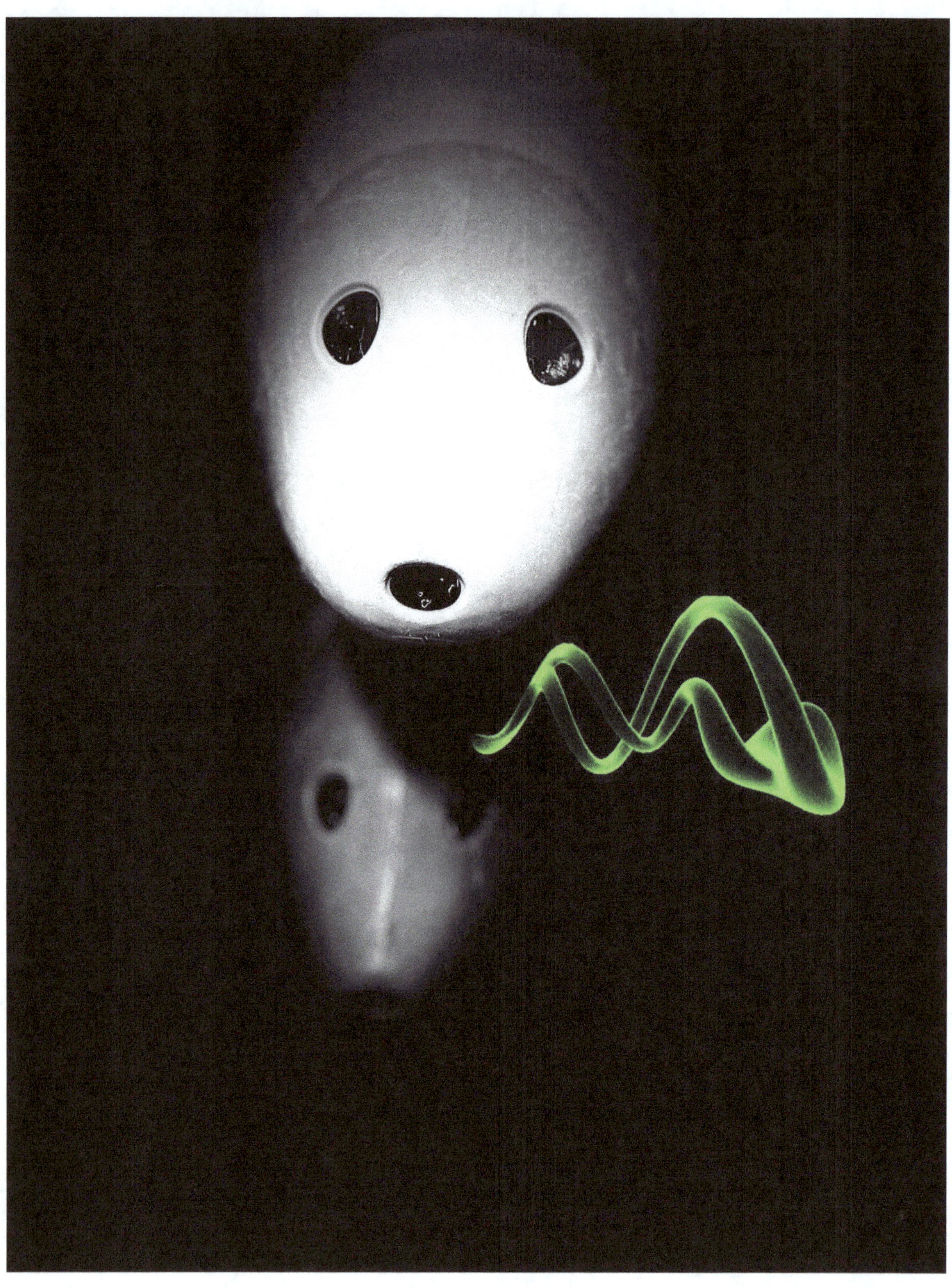

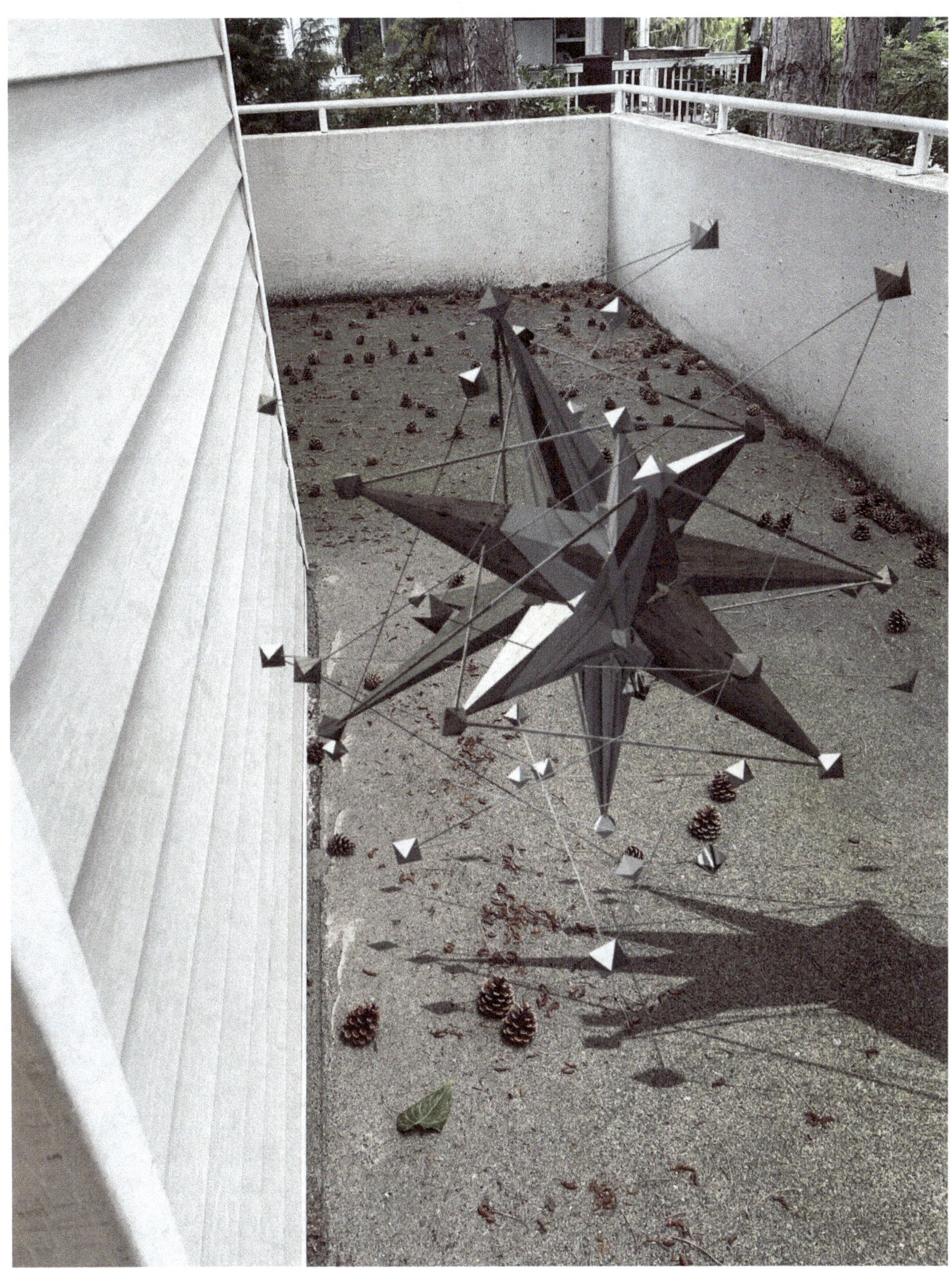

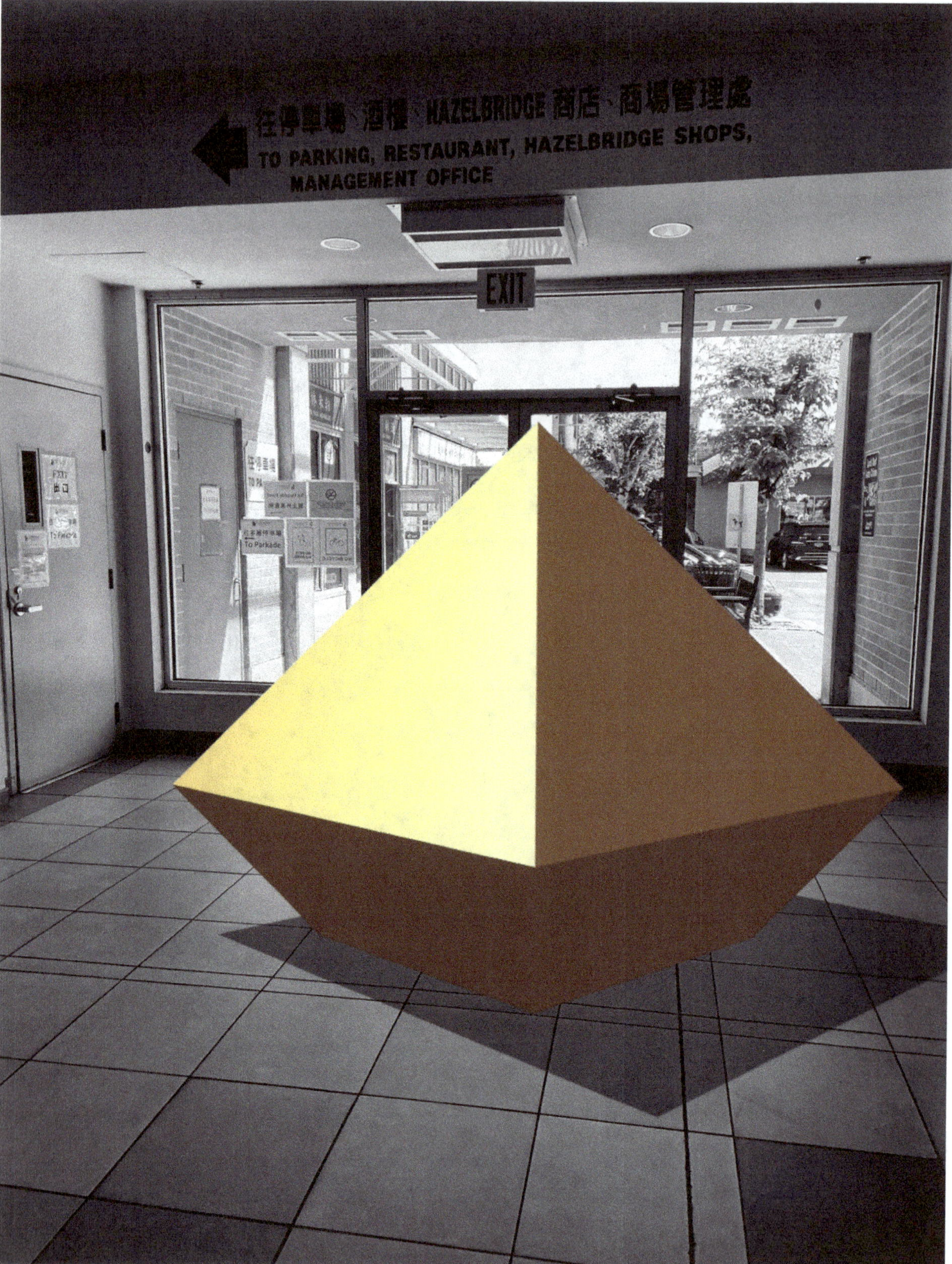
往停車場、酒樓、HAZELBRIDGE 商店、商場管理處
TO PARKING, RESTAURANT, HAZELBRIDGE SHOPS,
MANAGEMENT OFFICE
EXIT

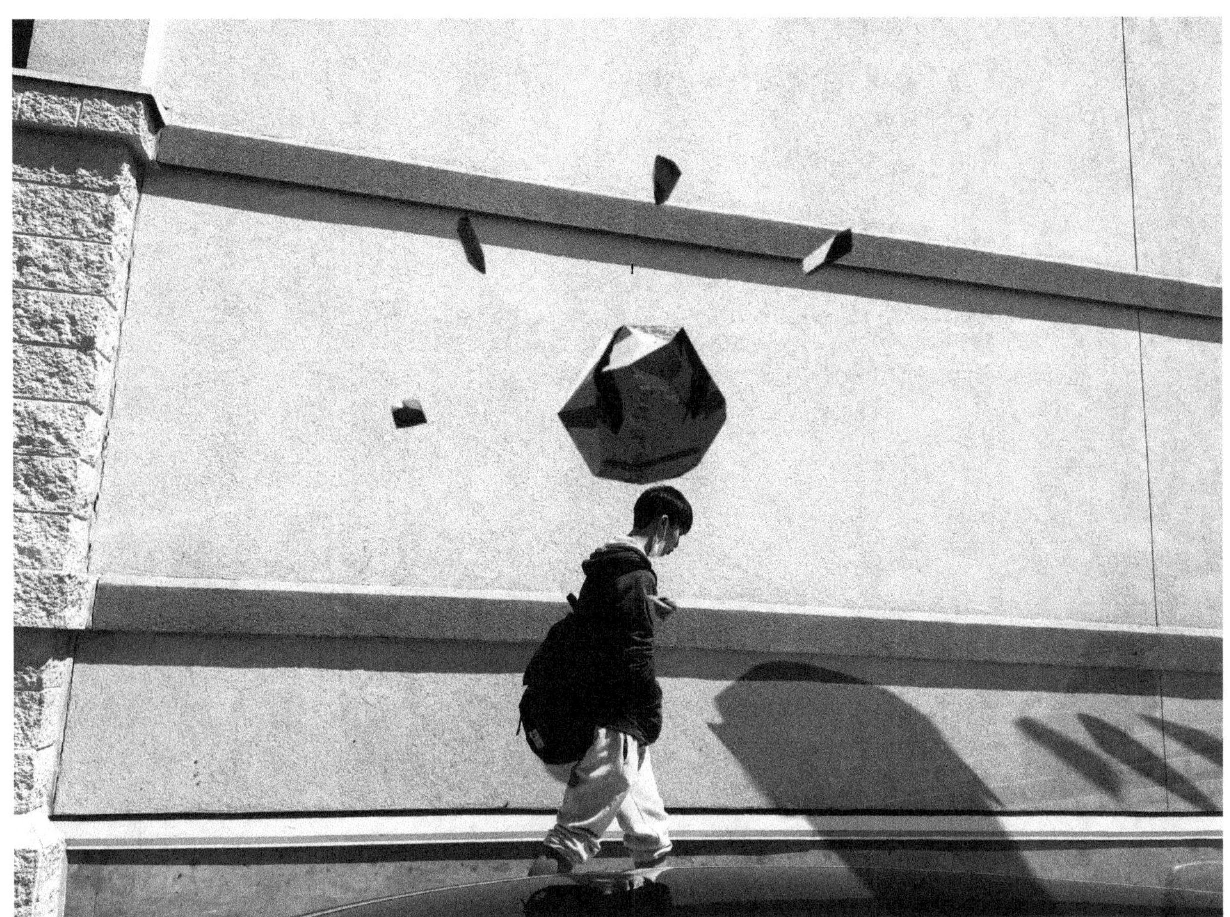

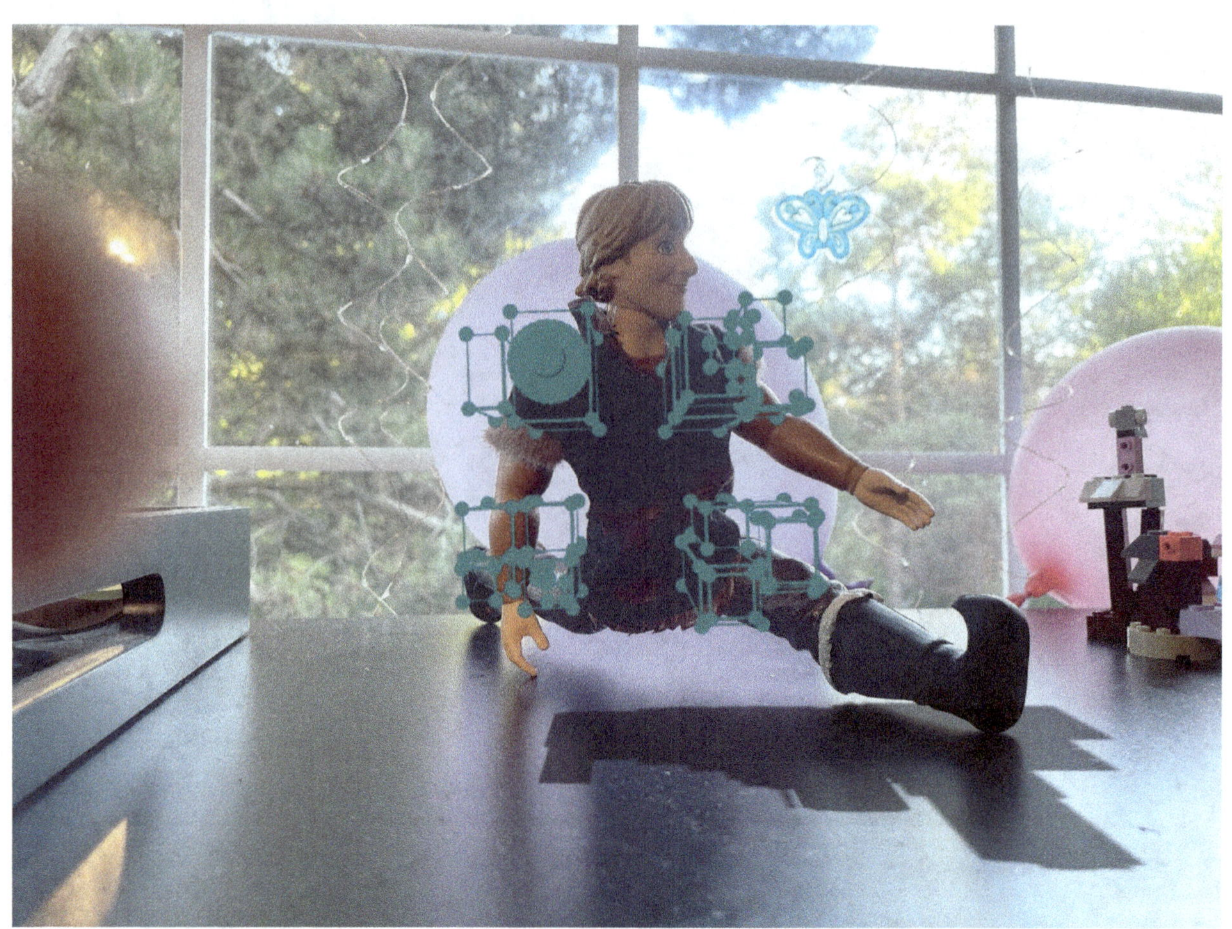

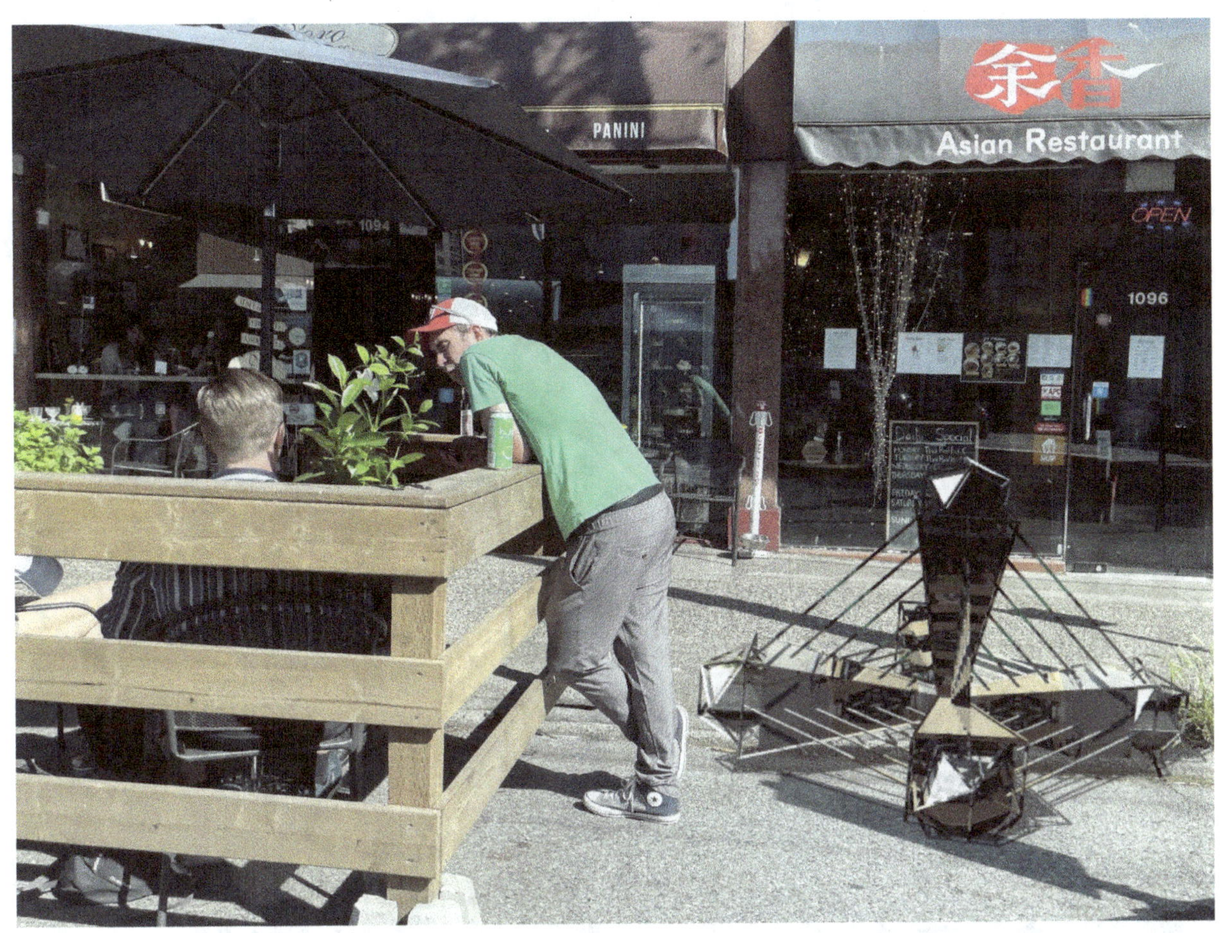
PANINI
1094
Asian Restaurant
OPEN
1096

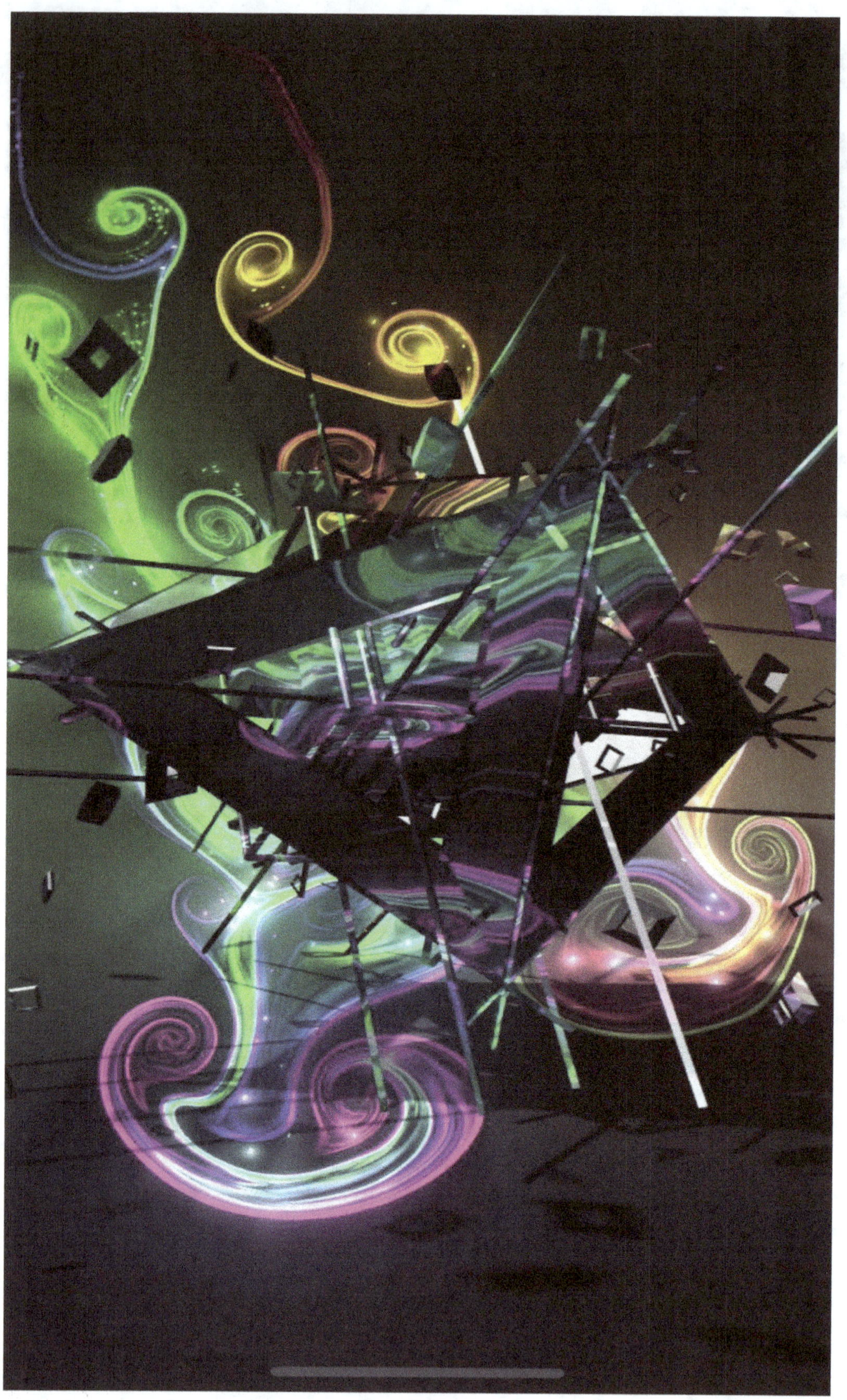

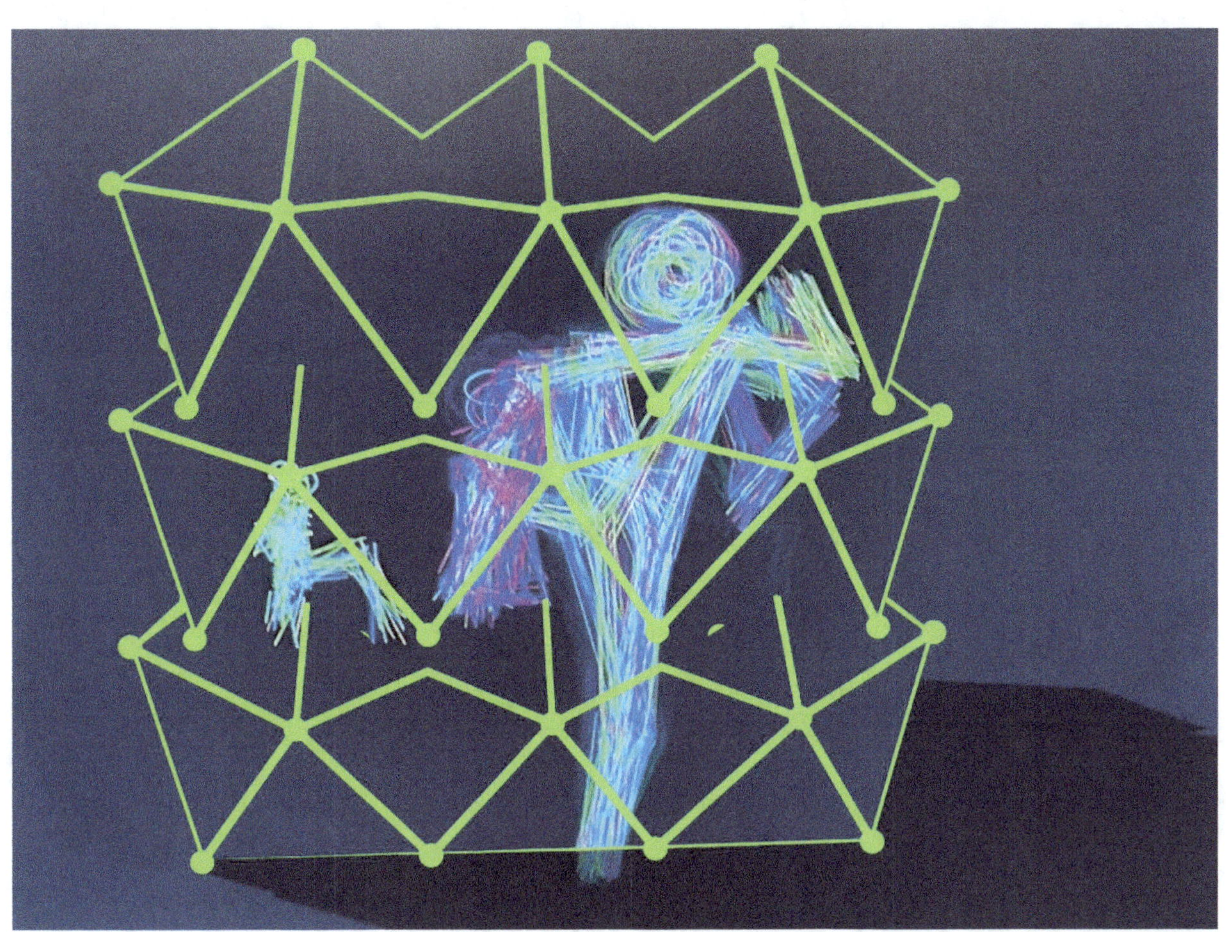

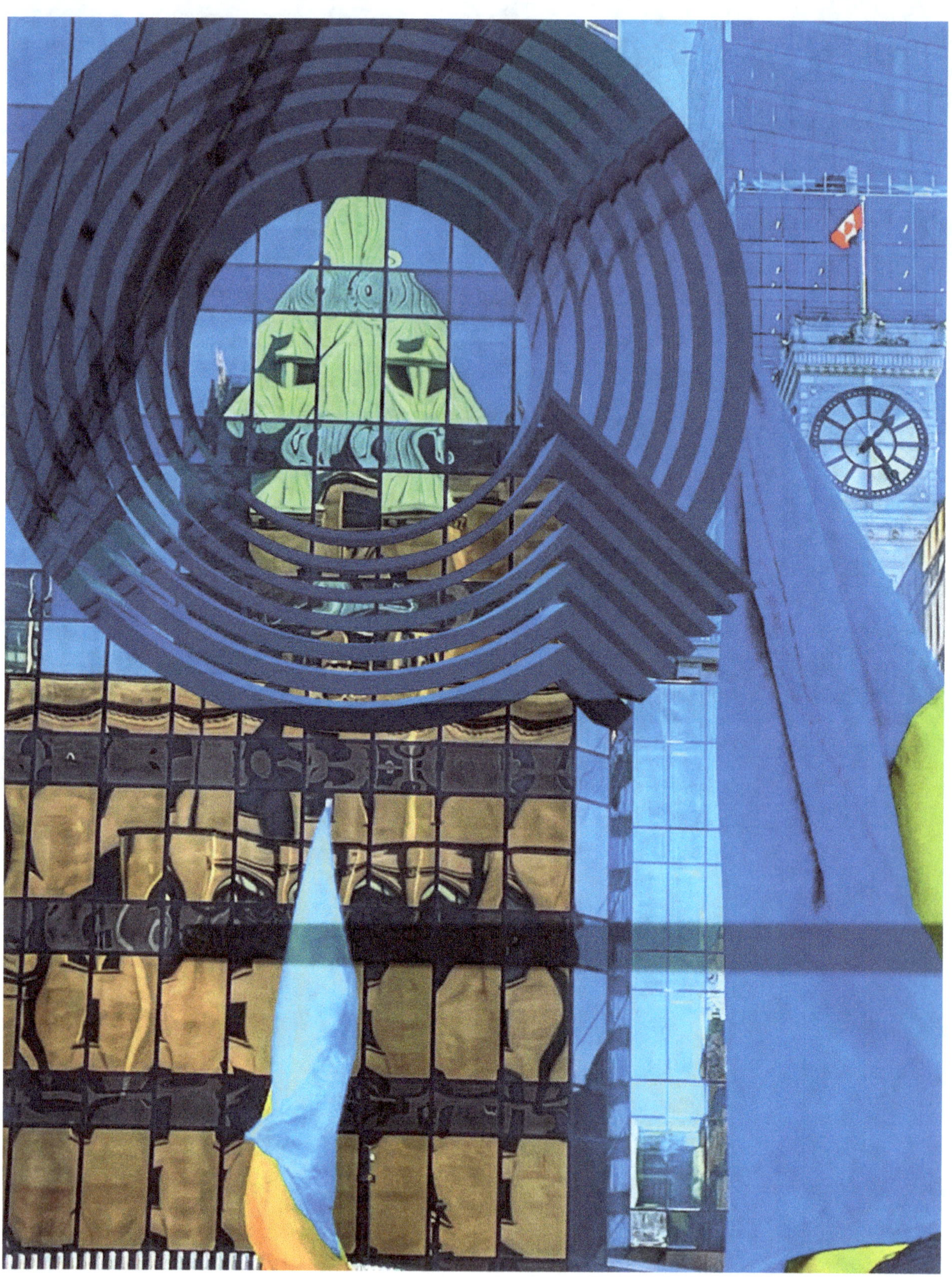

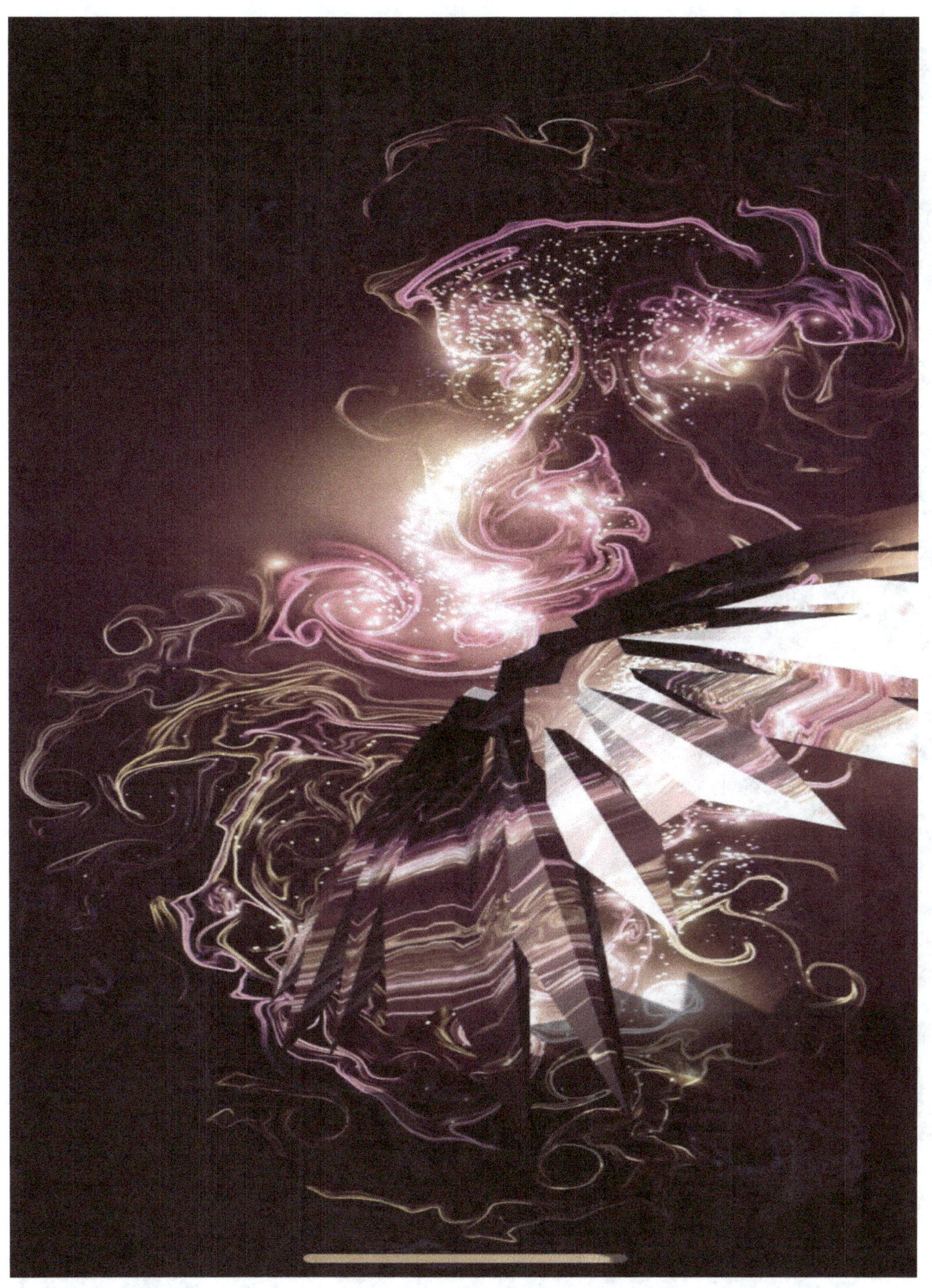

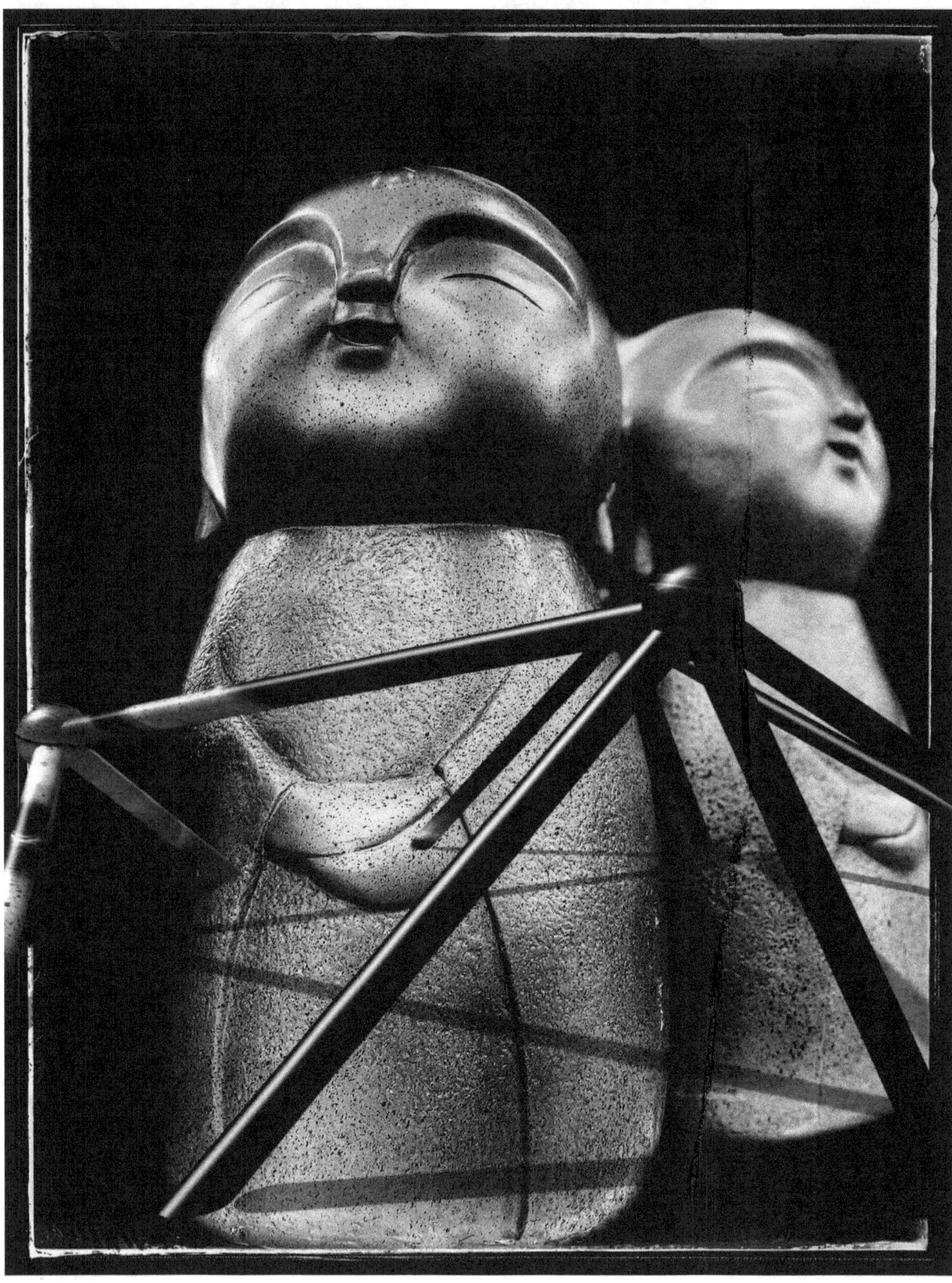

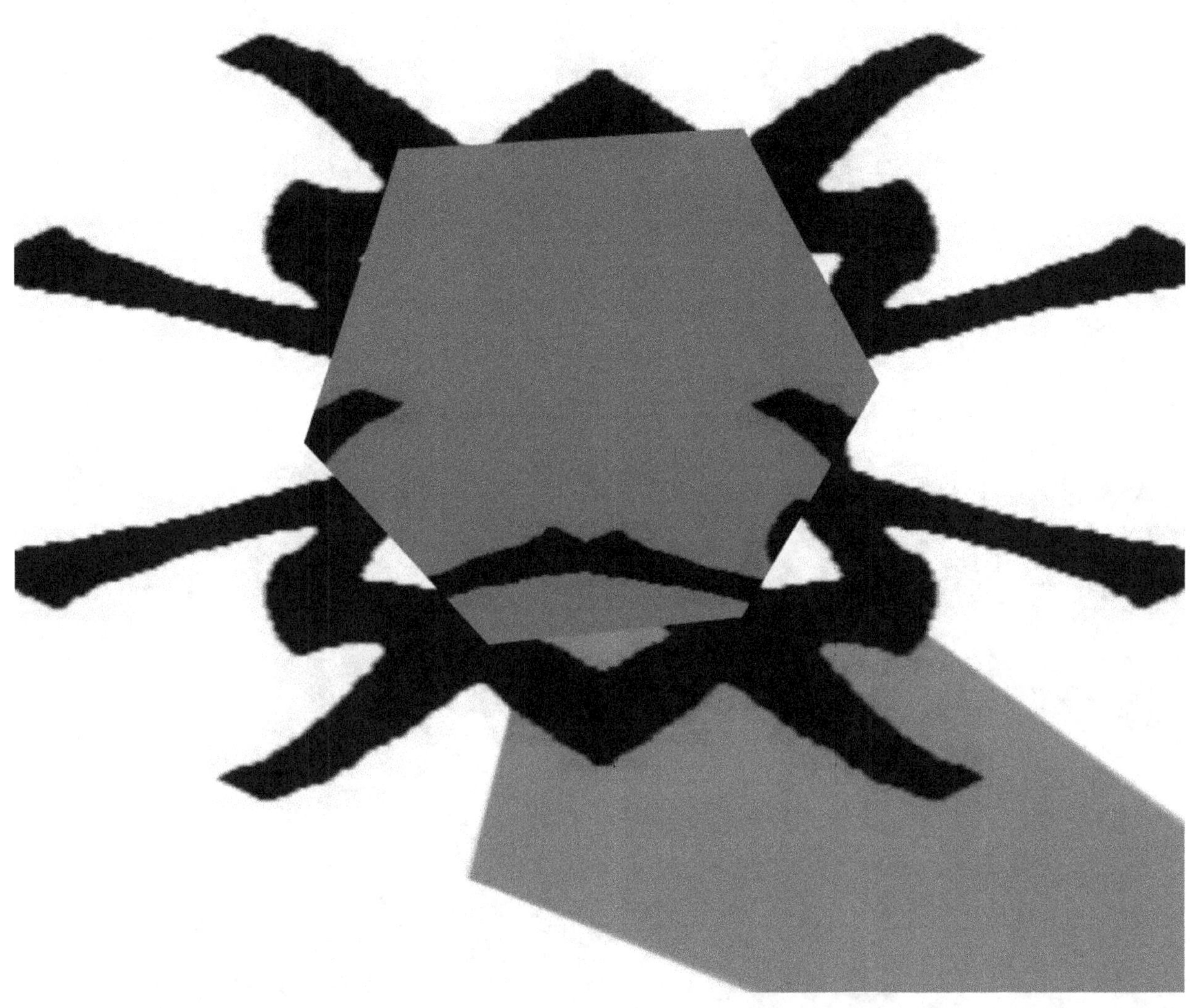

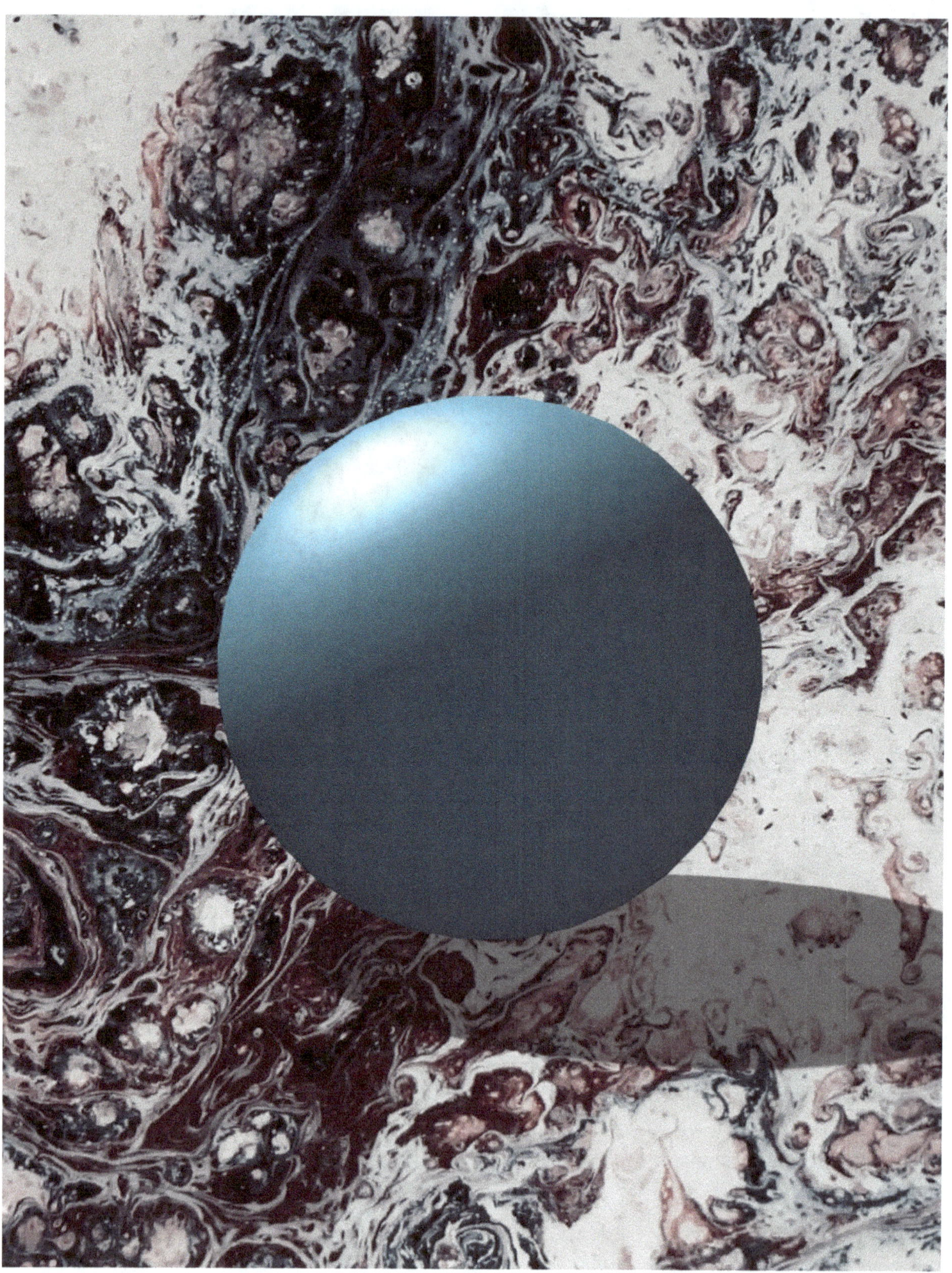

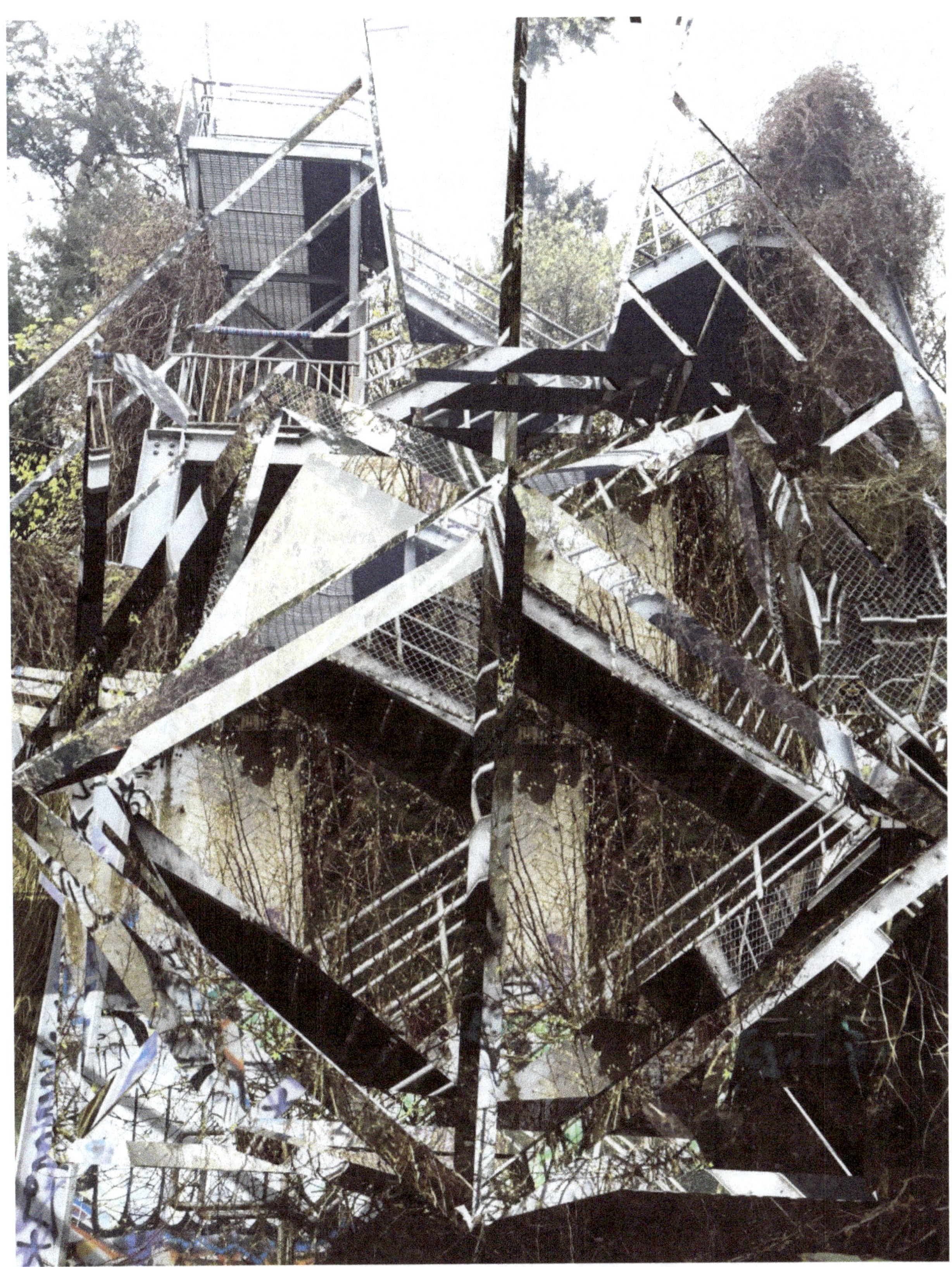

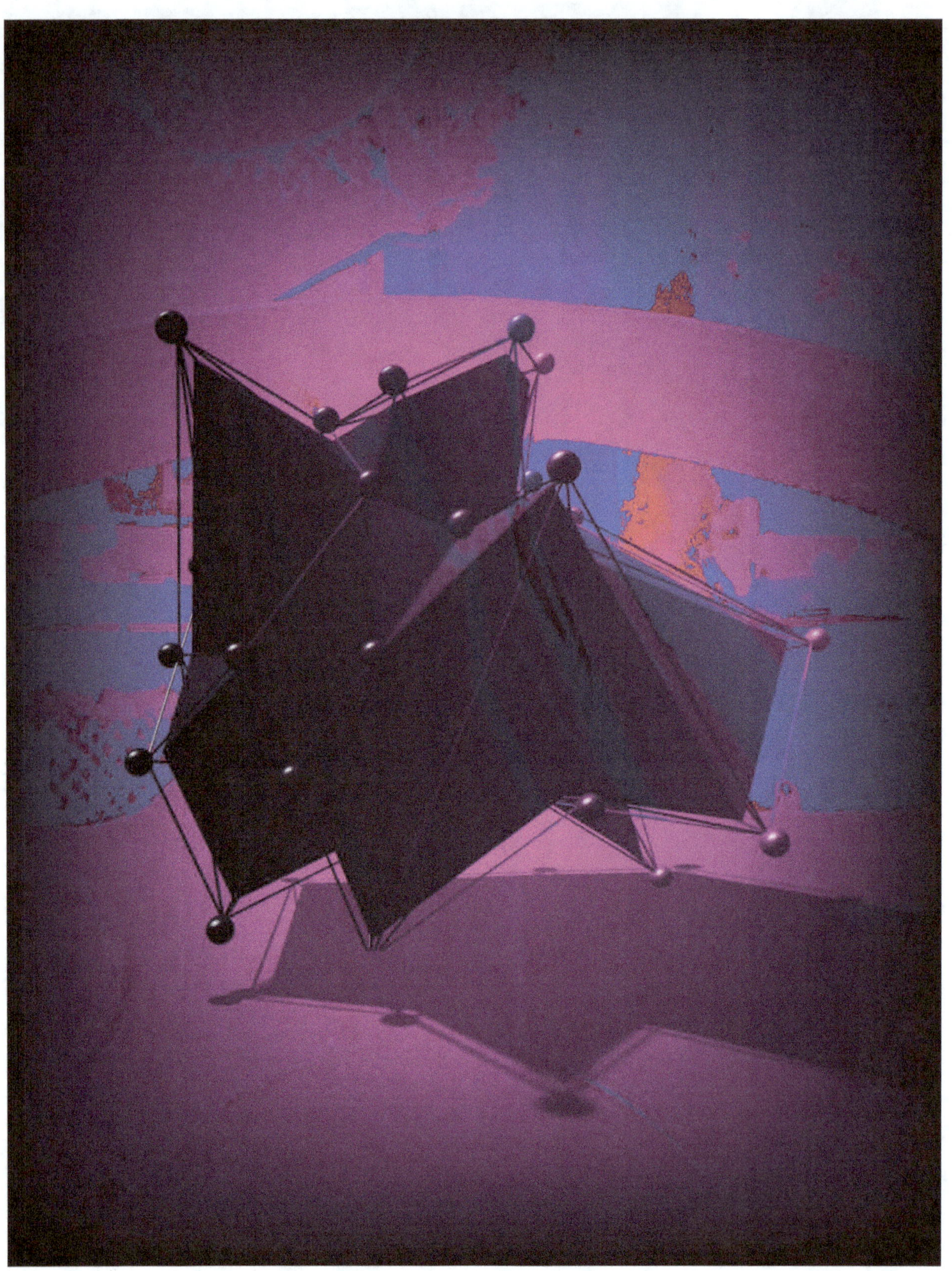

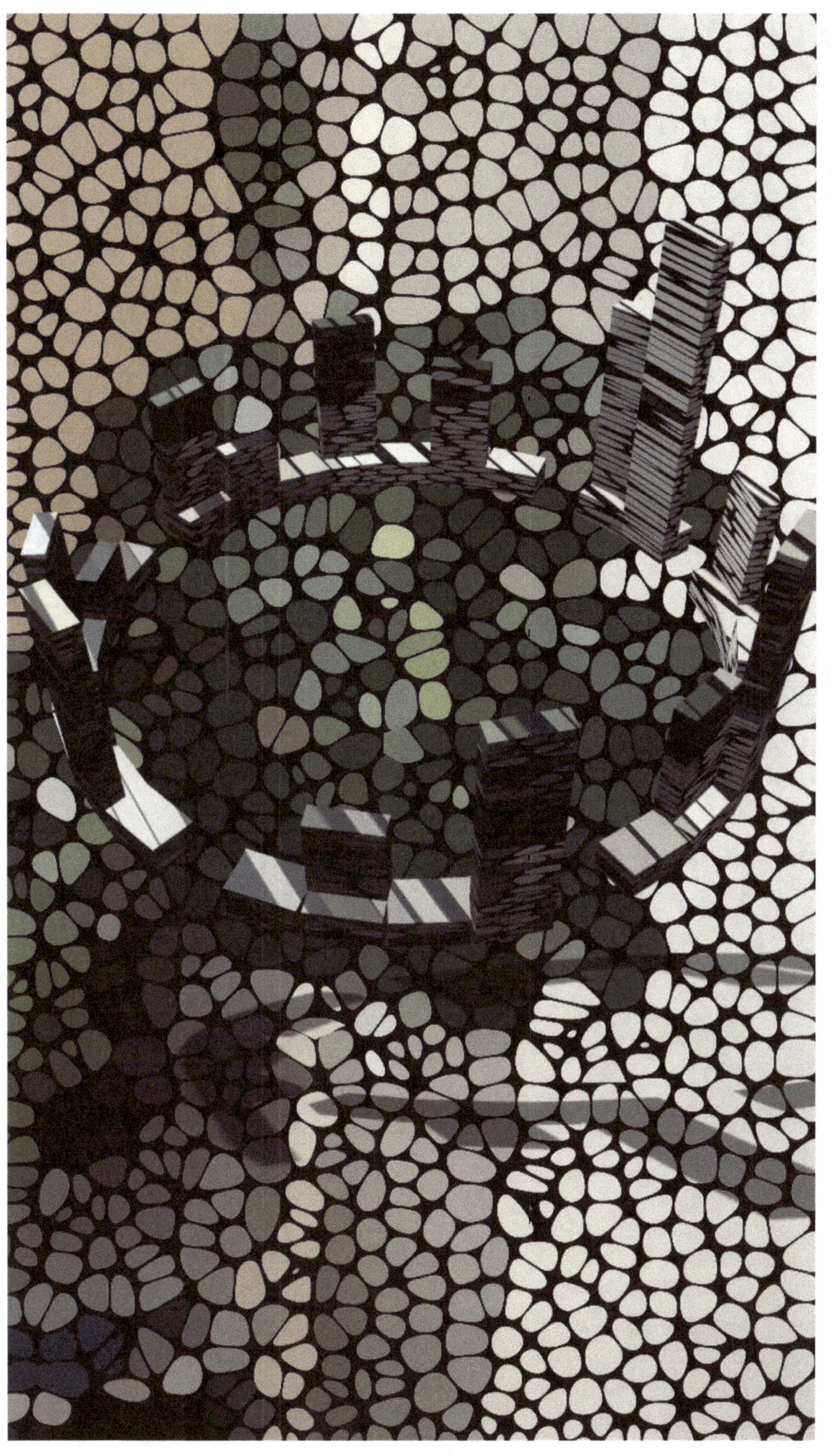

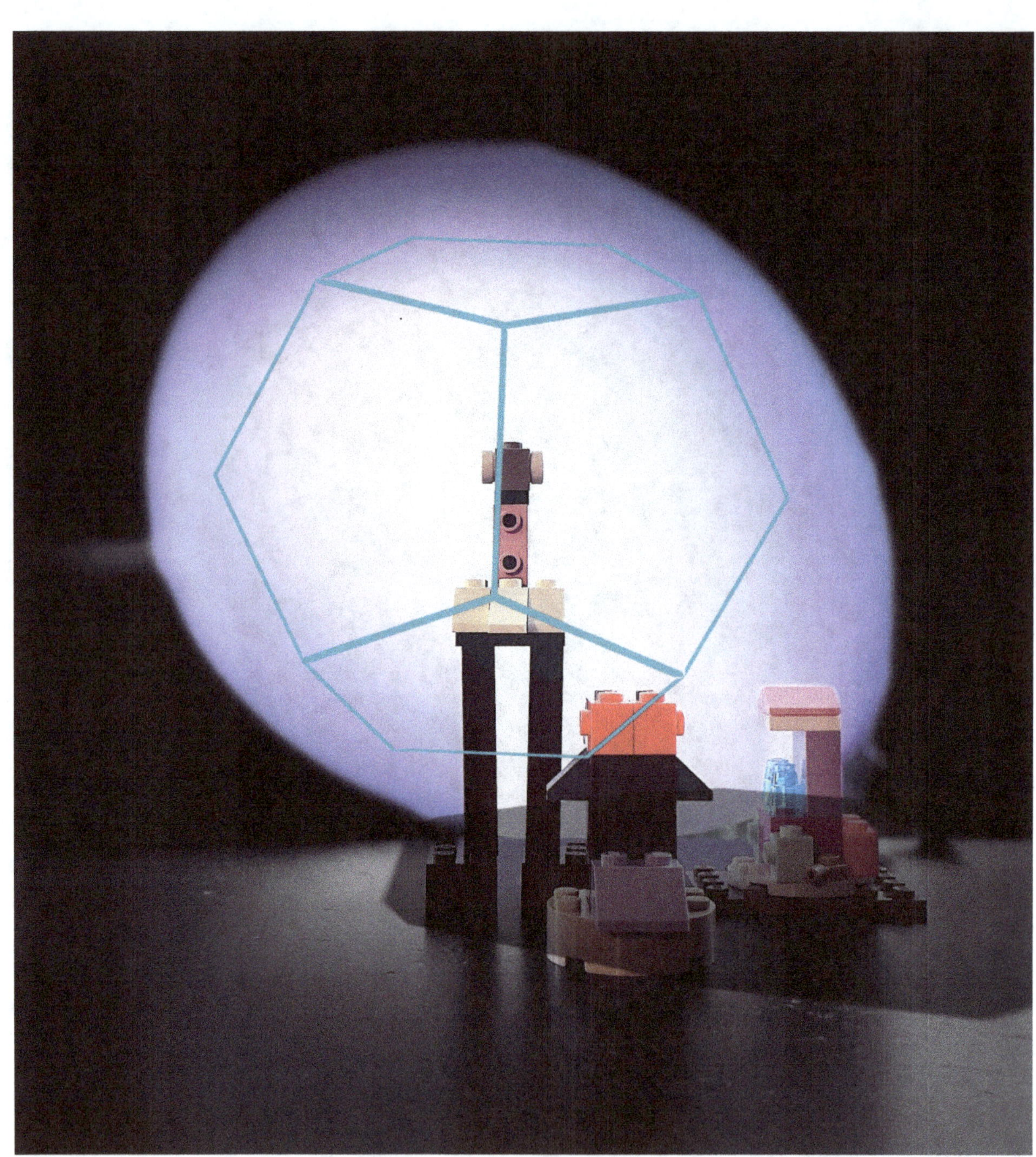

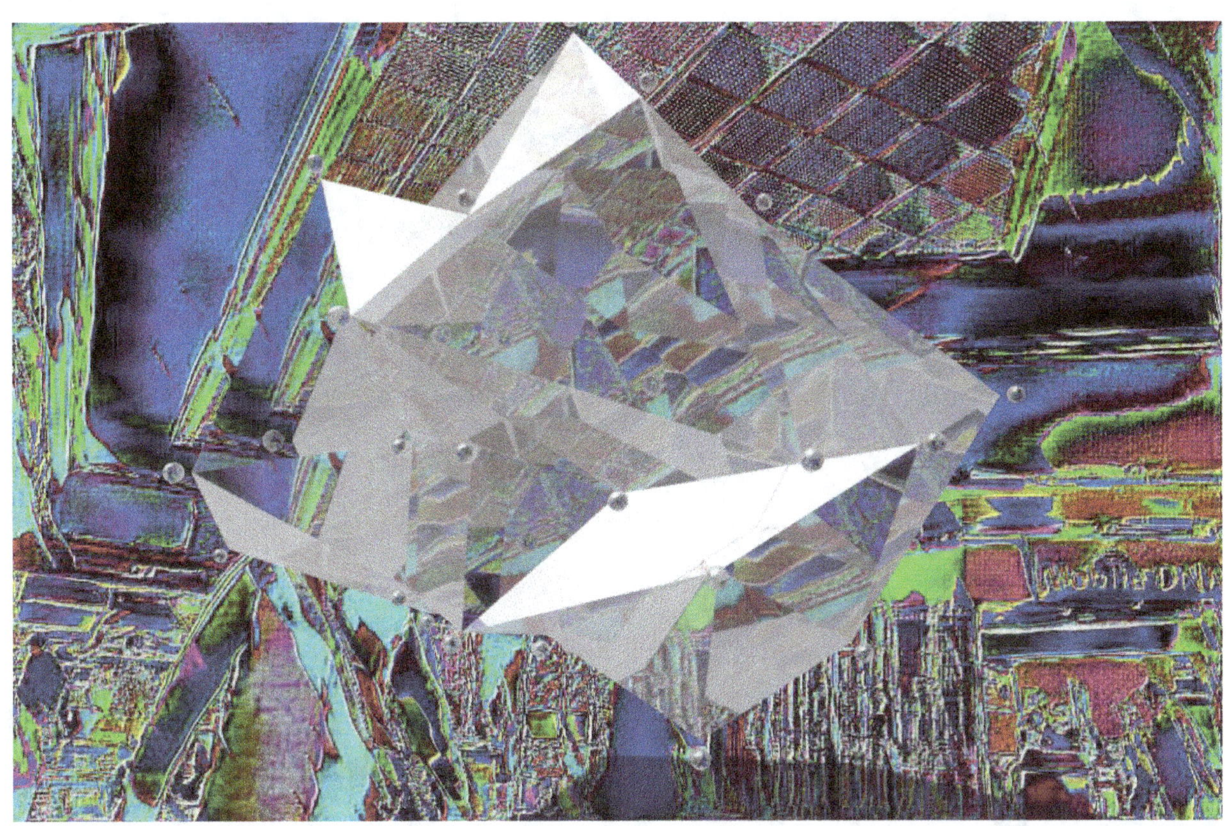

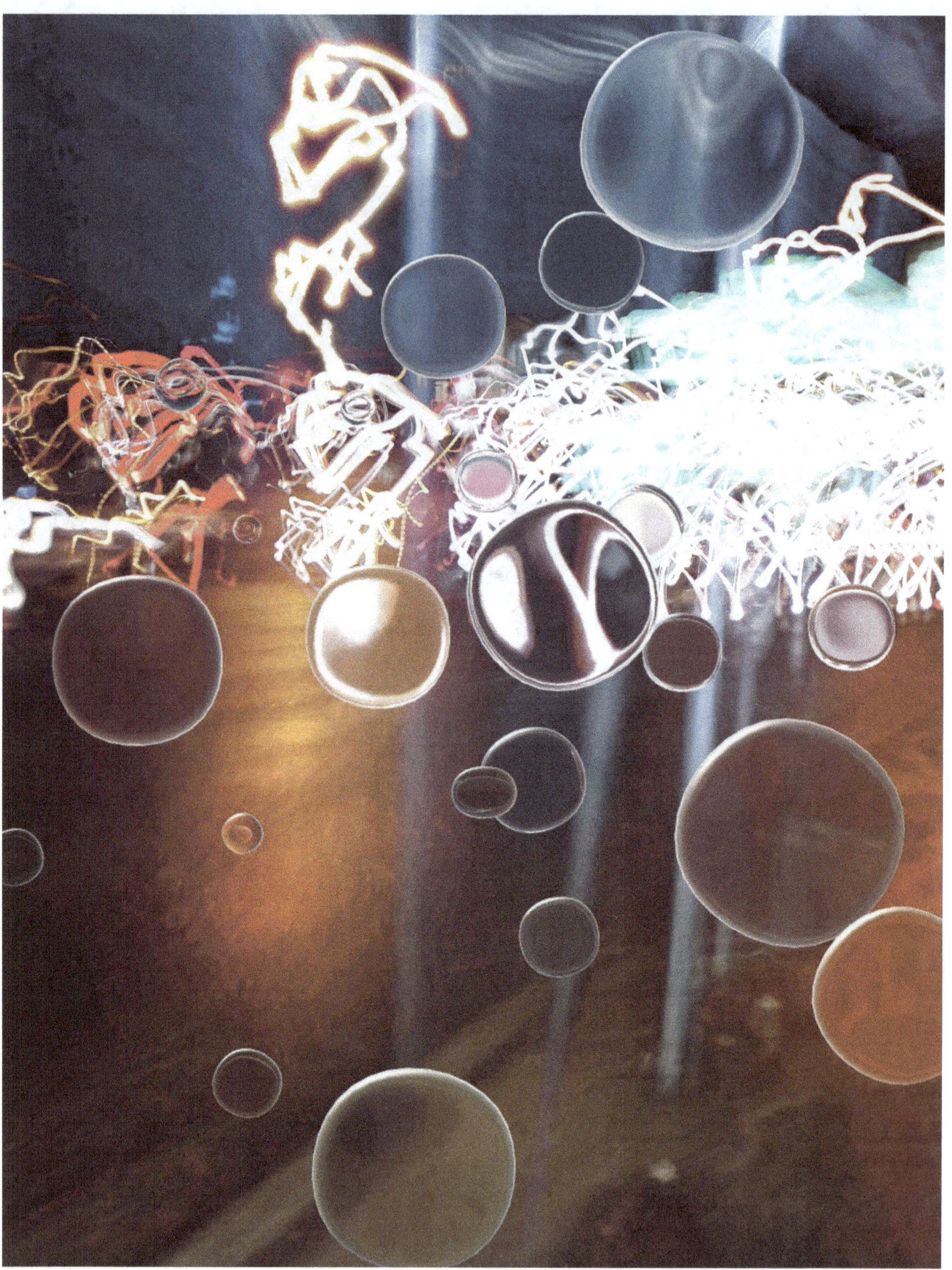

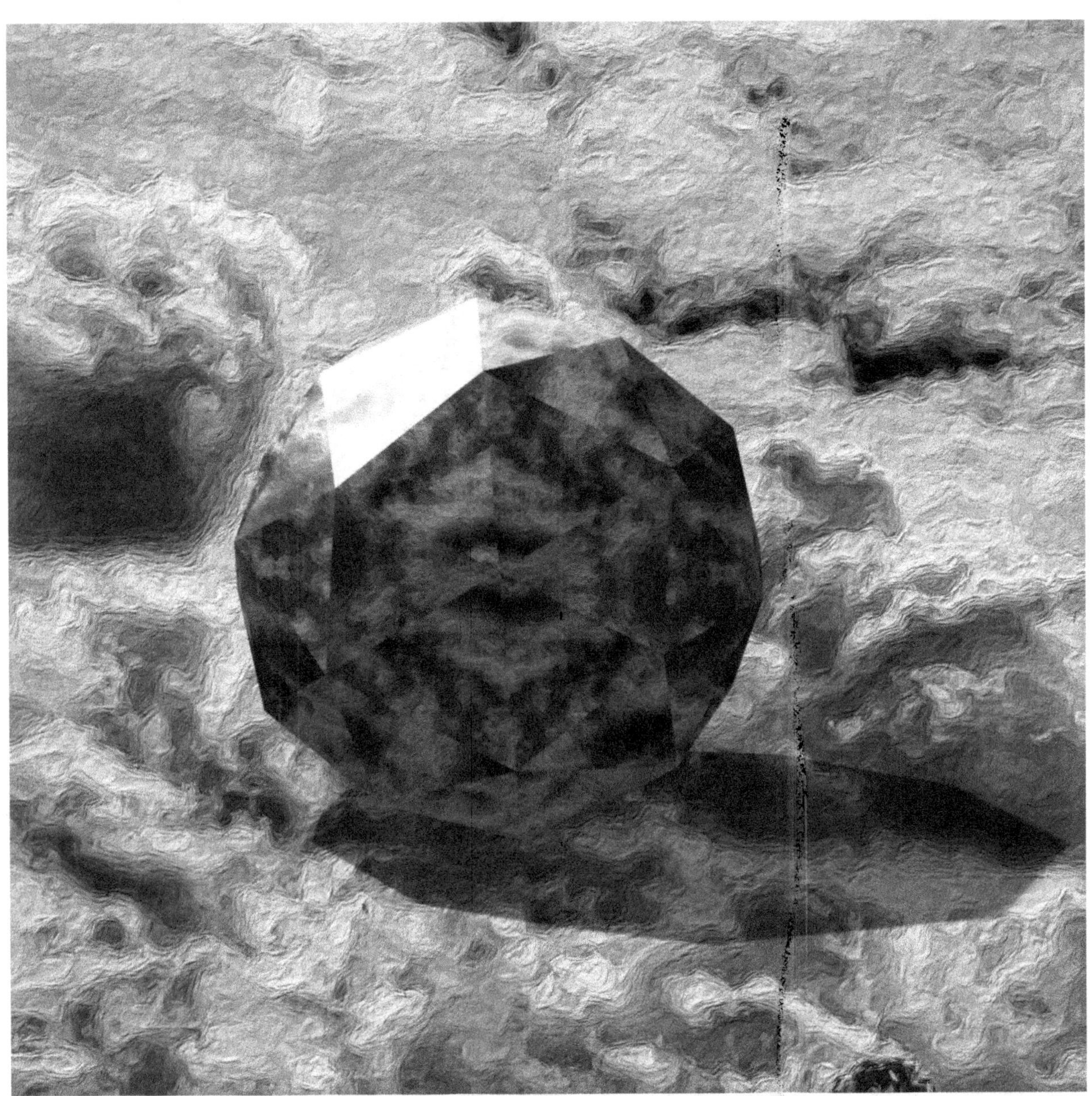

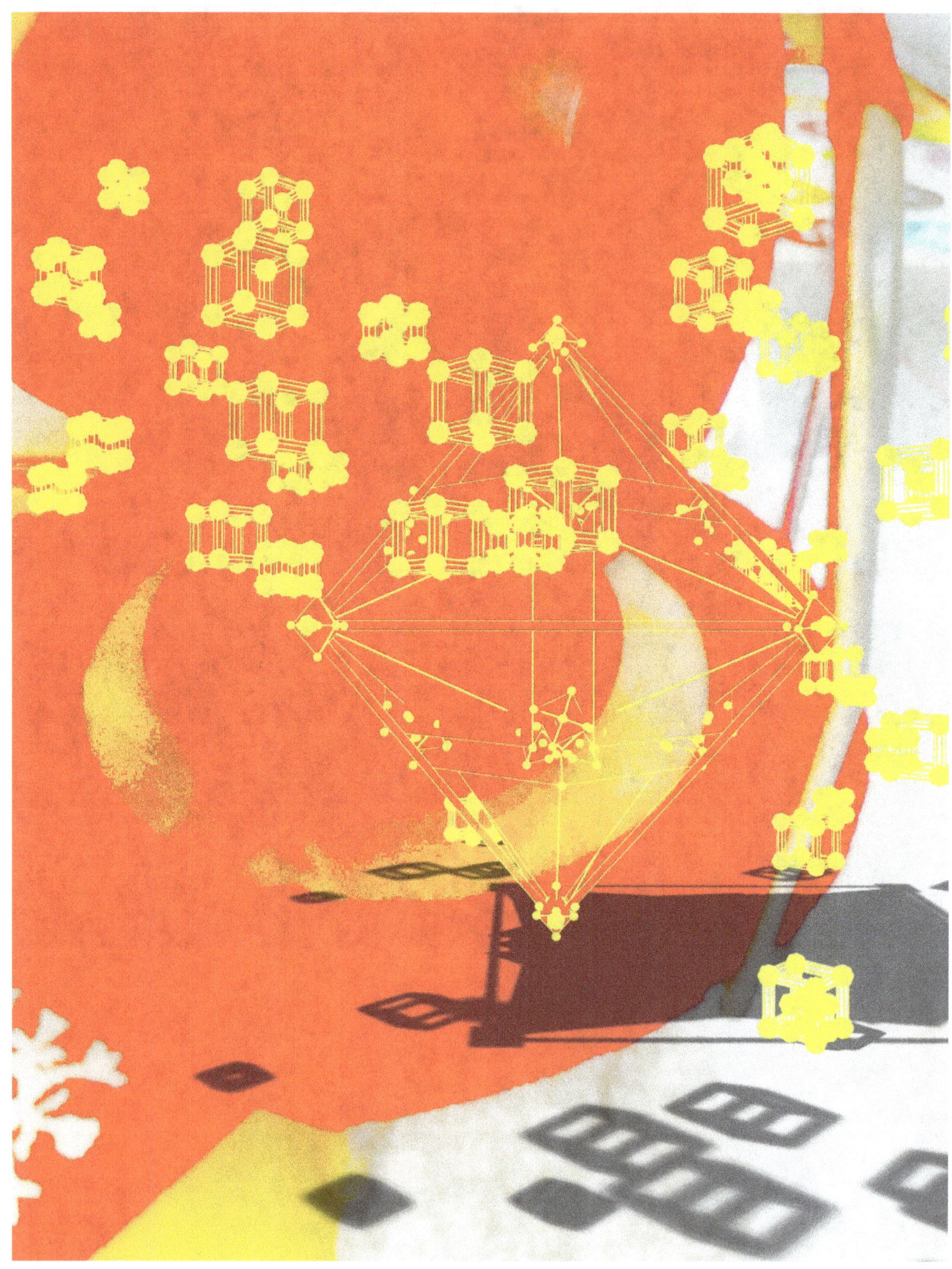

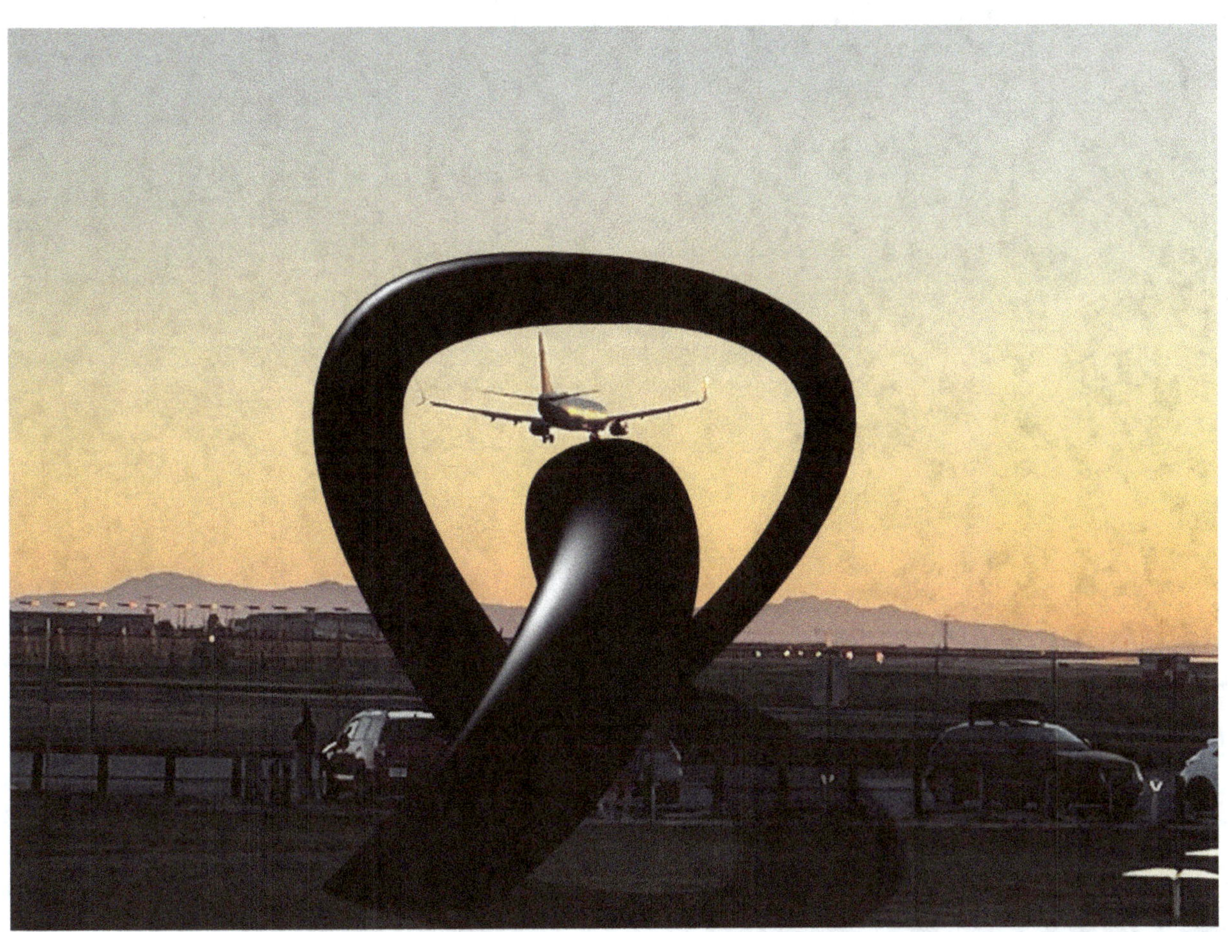

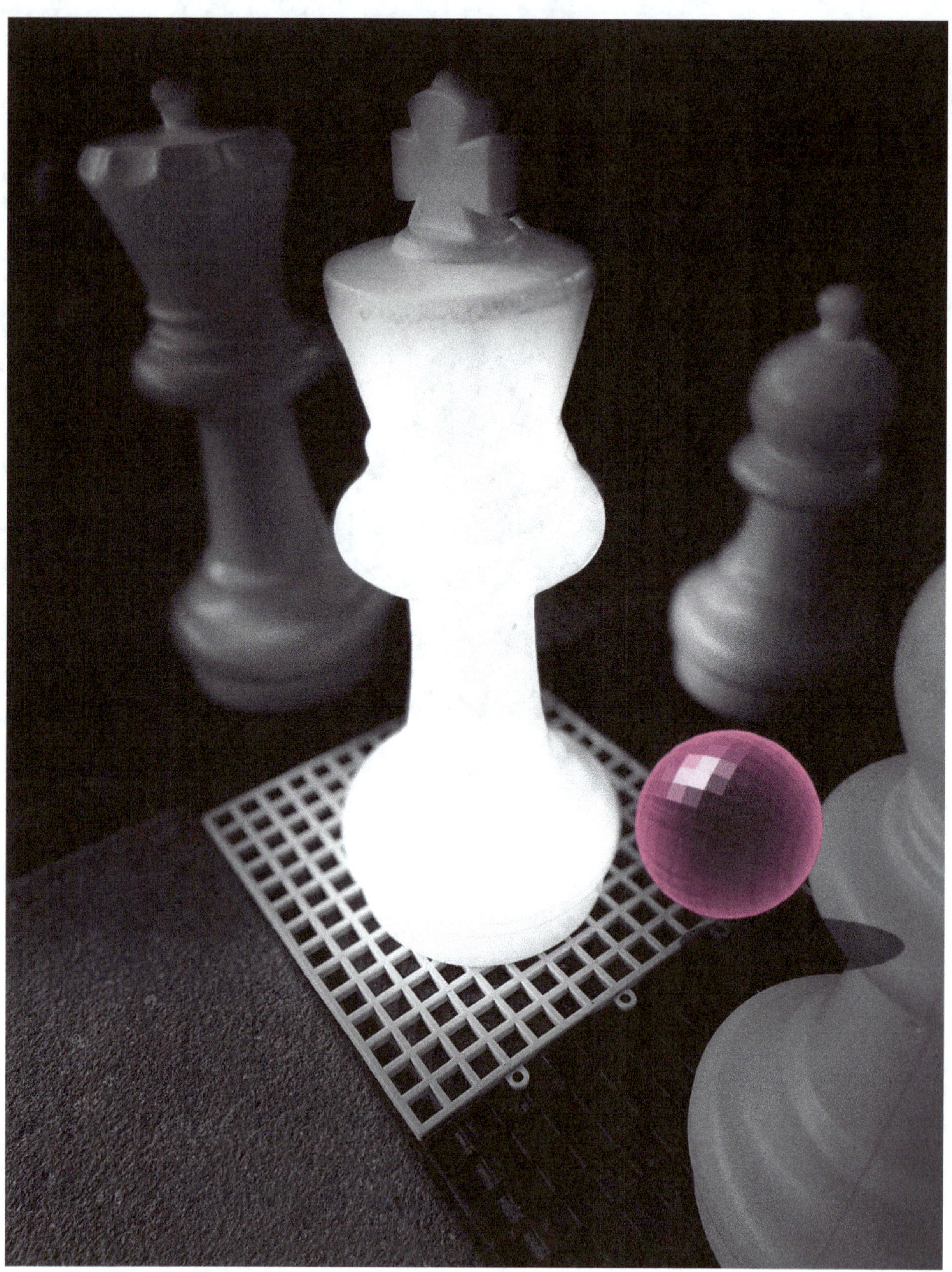

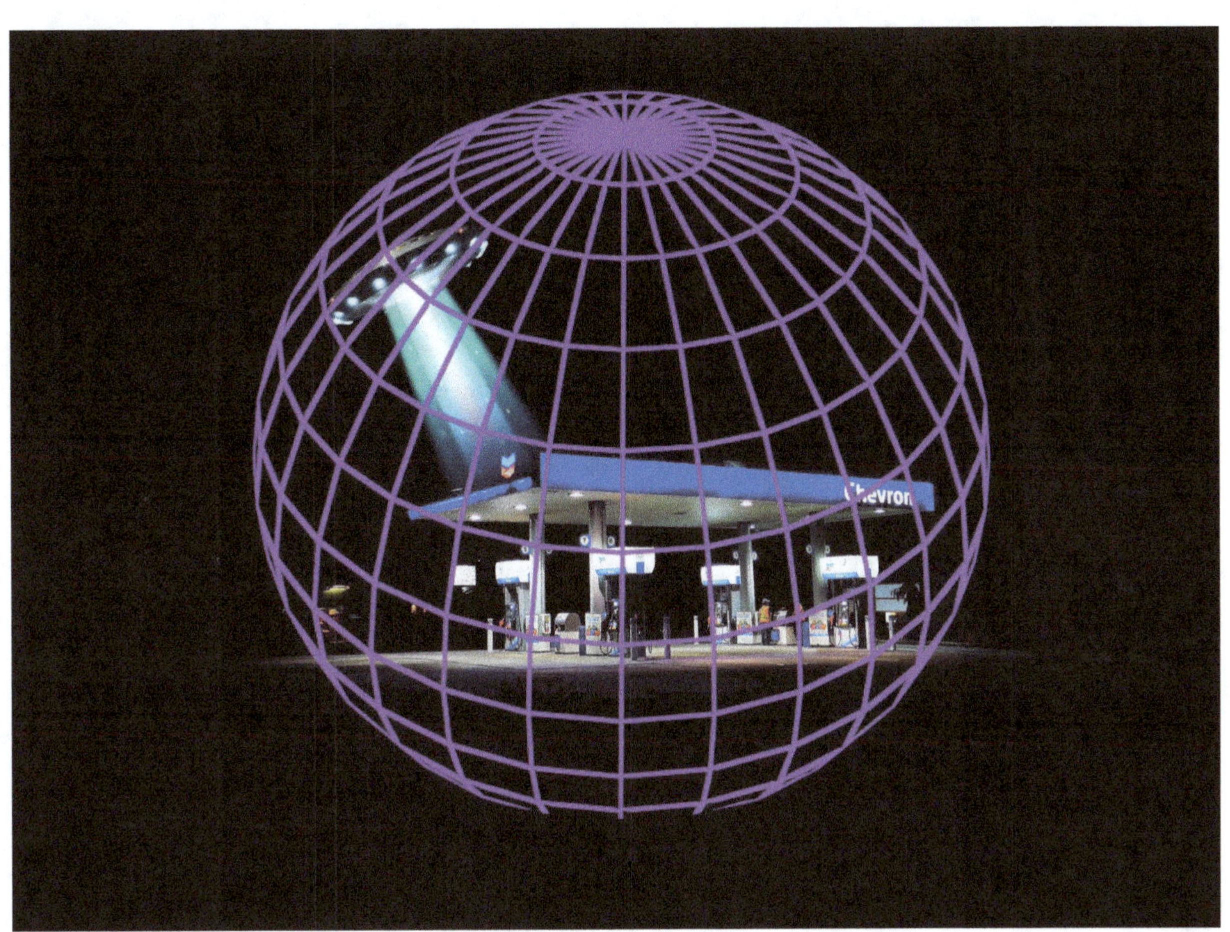